NEW SALAI

NEW

Quick,

SALADS
Healthy Recipes from Japan

Salads by **Shinko Shimizu**
Introduction by **Michio Kushi**
Photographs by **Masaya Suzuki**

KODANSHA INTERNATIONAL
Tokyo • New York • London

This book was made possible through the cooperation and invaluable assistance given by the following individuals in the capacities listed. Planning and editorial work were done by Chikurin Milbury and the staff of Kodansha International. Chikurin Milbury, a longtime food editor specializing in health and nutrition, provided the thinking that forms the basis for this book. Another veteran food editor, Masako Sugimoto, contributed her energy and writing skills to the project.

Shinko Shimizu created and arranged all the salads in the book, and Kyoko Furukawa provided the calorie count for each recipe.

The publisher wishes to give special thanks to the following companies and individuals who generously contributed cooking and serving utensils for use in the photographs appearing in this book: Tachikichi Inc., Gincho, Matsuya Department Store Co. Ltd., Wedgewood Japan, Orange House, Daimonji, Kyoji Nakatani, Masafumi Sekine, and Maruichi Setting Co. Ltd.

The publisher would also like to thank Mitoku Co. Ltd. for its support and the use of its natural products.

Note:
Calorie data are given for one serving and were calculated on the basis of the latest Japanese food composition tables.

In this book, 1 tablespoon equals 15 grams and one teaspoon equals 5 grams.

CONTENTS

INTRODUCTION

When I came to America from my native Japan in 1949, I found many things about the United States that were new and different. The thinking and lifestyle were almost totally opposite from those I was used to, and this made adapting to my surroundings an interesting adventure.

I was especially surprised by the difference in how food was presented, in particular how vegetables—raw and cooked—were prepared and served. I can remember trying to order vegetables and salads in restaurants. After several attempts, I soon realized that the selection was much narrower than what I had been accustomed to. I can remember my surprise when I ordered a salad and a plain wedge of lettuce appeared on my table. The selection of cooked vegetables was usually not much better. The boiled carrots and green peas that were sometimes available looked as if they had just come from a can. They were sadly lacking in vitality and seemed limp and tasteless.

I had grown up in the countryside and was used to eating a wide variety of raw and cooked vegetables. The preparation of vegetables and other natural foods was considered an art. My family enjoyed a wide selection of fresh vegetables, many grown in our own backyard, plus wild plants from the surrounding fields, mountains, and streams. They were carefully prepared and artistically served in a number of ways. Fresh vegetables were served raw, steamed, pickled, or boiled. Every farmhouse in the neighboring villages would serve an incredible variety of vegetables.

I grew up in this simple, rural environment, and despite the lean years and hard times brought on by the Second World War, I remember with great fondness the traditional Japanese foods served at home.

After twenty-five years in America, my wife Aveline and I visited Japan with our good friends, Gloria Swanson and her husband William Dufty. We visited several Buddhist temples and were served traditional Buddhist vegetarian cuisine. We were quite impressed with the refinement and artistry of this cuisine—and I was pleased to find these two aspects of that traditional cuisine wonderfully represented in the salads in this book.

With a proper understanding, our daily food can be our best medicine. Over the past thirty-five years, my wife and I have developed macrobiotic natural living throughout North America, Europe, and Central America by teaching how the daily diet affects our energy, health, and vitality as well as the mental and spiritual quality of life.

The natural food movement, which has spread throughout the world, was started more than twenty years ago in Boston with the support and efforts of our friends and students. In a discussion that took place at our home in Brookline, the term "natural" was selected, in part to distinguish natural foods from what were then known as "health" foods and were for the main part dietary supplements. The term was first used in America with the establishment of Erewhon, the first natural food store, in Boston. Now natural food has become a part of the mainstream of the food industry in western countries.

The recent public emphasis on diet as a means to prevent chronic illness has also been influenced by macrobiotic education. Currently many public health agencies are recommending a way of eating that is similar to that of macrobiotics for the prevention of major illnesses. We have also known many individuals who overcame a serious illness and recovered their health through practicing macrobiotics. The idea of approaching cooking as an art, so essential to macrobiotics, is similar to the approach in this volume.

Not all the ingredients used in this book—brown sugar and eggs, for example—are recommended for those recovering from an illness or maintaining optimum health through macrobiotics. However, we can all learn from and appreciate the aesthetic approach to the preparation and presentation of dishes offered in this book. Macrobiotic cooks can readily adapt this style and approach by substituting the most healthful ingredients. They will find many wonderful ideas to make their cooking more creative, beautiful, and varied.

The art of cooking is the epitome of human creation. It reflects the whole personality of the cook—physical constitution, mental condition, and spiritual attainments as well as the cook's economic and aesthetic taste. Cooking continuously adapts to fit man's biological, social, and spiritual evolution and reflects the constantly changing social and natural environment. It deals directly with human life, influencing and producing an individual's health, mind, and spirit as well as his character and way of thinking, and even can be said to determine his destiny.

Therefore, the art of cooking is the art of life. He who adroitly manages the philosophical, spiritual, practical, technical, economical, social, emotional, and sensorial aspects of cooking will govern his future and his family's happiness, and help prepare for one peaceful world.

I hope everyone with an interest in these fresh salads from the Japanese tradition will enjoy, adapt, and use the methods presented in this book. I am grateful to everyone who worked on this book and made it available.

Michio Kushi
Brookline, Massachusetts
February 1986

MICHIO KUSHI Since coming to the United States over thirty years ago, Michio Kushi has helped thousands of people achieve physical, psychological, and spiritual health and well-being through macrobiotics. Inspired by George Ohsawa's dietary teachings, Kushi and his wife Aveline began to study applications of traditional Eastern philosophy and medicine to modern society and its problems. In the early 1960s their studies led to the founding of Erewhon, the first distributor of macrobiotic and natural foods in the United States. In 1970 the Kushis founded the *East West Journal*, a monthly magazine on nutrition, health, and natural lifestyles. This was followed two years later by the creation of the East West Foundation for macrobiotics education and research. In 1978 they established the Kushi Institute of Boston to train macrobiotic teachers, counselors, and cooks. During the last twenty years, Kushi and his wife have given lectures and seminars on the macrobiotic way of life throughout North and Central America, Europe, and Asia. Kushi has published over two dozen books, including *Natural Healing through Macrobiotics*, *Macrobiotic Diet*, *Cancer Prevention Diet*, and *Diet for a Strong Heart*.

BEAUTIFUL SALADS

The beauty of Japanese salads is their simplicity—a simplicity born of labor and invention that raise the end product to the level of art. The secret is more than just a pretty color scheme. A great salad draws out the characteristics of each ingredient and then blends them harmoniously. Color, taste, shape, and texture are all part of the artful synthesis. Nonetheless, the key to successful salads is not the privileged property of professional chefs. Anyone with a basic aptitude for food can create attractive salads with a Japanese touch.

A First Course Salad

Shrimp and *Wakame* Seaweed with Vinegared Egg Yolk Dressing, page 69.

Salads for a Buffet

Clockwise from extreme left: Cauliflower with Sea Urchin Mayonnaise, page 69; Broccoli with *Konbu* Tea Dressing, page 70; Turnips and Apricots in Sweet Vinegar Dressing, page 70; Tomato Appetizer, page 71; Daikon Radish and Kiwi Fruit Salad, page 71.

Salads as Appetizers

From top to bottom: Mountain Yam with Green
Seaweed Flakes, page 72; Okra with Flavorful Cod Roe
Dressing, page 71; Red Shell with Mustard-Vinegar-
Miso Dressing, page 72.

From top to bottom: Orange Baskets, page 73;
Avocado and Shrimp Salad, page 73; Smoked Salmon
with Rape Flower Dressing, page 73.

Main Dish Salads

Counterclockwise from upper left: Rice Salad, page 74; Clams with Ginger-Soy Dressing, page 74; White Fish Salad, page 75.

Portable Salads

Counterclockwise from top: Cabbage and Carrot Layers, page 75; Salted Turnips with Raisins and Lemon, page 76; Sardines in Nanban Vinegar-Ginger Dressing, page 76.

HEALTHY SALADS

The raw materials of Japanese salads are the raw materials of a healthy diet—tofu and beans for protein; mineral-rich seaweed; roots and tubers full of the vitamins and enzymes that prevent illness; low-calorie, high-fiber mushrooms; and the balanced nutrition of whole grains. This goodness is brought to life with a mild dressing flavored with miso or soy sauce, or perhaps a variation seasoned with pickled plums or sesame. This book points out some basics—healthy vegetables and suitable dressings. From these building blocks, devise your own salad creations.

Light Salads

Counterclockwise from upper right: Lotus Root with Pickled Plum Dressing, page 77; Green Pepper with Chopped Sesame Dressing, page 78; Tomato and Watercress Salad with Japanese-style Dressing, page 77.

Root Vegetable Salads

Clockwise from extreme left: Fried Potatoes with Hot Cucumber-Daikon Dressing, page 79; Burdock and Sesame Salad, page 78; Daikon Radish and Carrots with *Shiso* Dressing, page 78.

Mushroom Salads

Clockwise from upper left; *Shimeji* Mushroom and Spinach Salad, page 79; Shiitake Mushroom and Daikon Sprout Salad, page 80; *Enoki* Mushrooms with Daikon-Cod Roe Dressing, page 80.

Tofu Salads

From top to bottom: Butterhead Lettuce with Miso-Flavored Tofu, page 80; Deep-fried Tofu Salad, page 81; Chilled Tofu, page 82.

20

Soybean Salads

From top to bottom: Green Soybeans Boiled on the Stalk, page 83; Soybeans and *Hijiki* Seaweed with *Wasabi*-Soy Mayonnaise, page 82.

Noodle and Rice Salads

From top to bottom: Rice Salad with Western Vegetables, page 85; Saifun Noodle and Egg Thread Salad, page 86.

From top to bottom: *Somen* Noodle Salad, page 84; *Kuzu* Noodle Salad, page 84; Japanese-style Spaghetti Salad, page 83.

Seaweed Salads

Clockwise from upper left: *Hijiki* Seaweed with Vinegar-Soy Dressing, page 87; Cabbage and *Wakame* Seaweed with Mild Soy Dressing, page 87; Three-Color *Tosakanori* Seaweed with Miso-Egg Yolk Dressing, page 86.

BEFORE YOU BEGIN

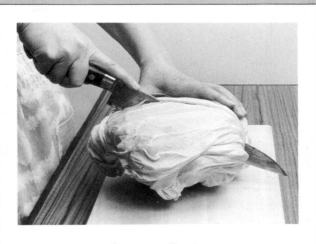

Cutting Basics

Japanese cooking is said to begin with the knife. Though some of the cutting techniques may initially appear difficult, as you practice the basics, you will soon see the art and logic of the more advanced methods. Choose a knife that fits your hand and the work to be done, and learn to feel comfortable with it.

The Basic Knife

Knives vary in size and shape depending on their purpose, but for general use in any kitchen, a standard, medium-size chef's knife is best. The blade should be 7–9 inches (18–22 cm) long. The relative merits of carbon versus stainless steel blades are often debated, but stainless steel knives are generally more readily available and easier to care for. If you intend to add just one other knife besides this basic all-purpose knife, get a short paring knife for peeling fruits and vegetables.

Holding the Knife

When cutting hard or thick objects, grip the handle firmly with the outer three fingers of your hand and more lightly with your thumb and index finger. Gripping tightly with all five fingers tires the arm and prevents a smooth cutting motion.

You can also extend your index finger and lay it on the back of the blade. This method allows you to control the direction and amount of pressure being applied and is the best way to chop finely or perform other delicate tasks.

Cutting Posture

Place the cutting board parallel with the counter. To prevent it from slipping, wet a kitchen towel, wring it out thoroughly, and spread it under the board. Stand about the width of your hand away from the counter. Stand up straight and step back with your right foot so your body is at a 45° angle to the cutting board. Cut with the knife perpendicular to the cutting board.

Basic Cutting Techniques

Different parts of the knife are used to make different cuts. The following section introduces the basic uses of the tip, middle, and base of the blade.

If you are a novice at chopping, work slowly and deliberately. As you gain experience you can increase the pace.

Drawing Cut

For this method, only the tip of the knife is used, and the base stays well above the cutting surface. It is convenient for slicing long objects in straight pieces or cutting squid (see p. 54) and other foods in even strips.

Pushing Cut

When cutting cabbage, onions, or other dense vegetables, the middle of the blade is used. As you cut, push slightly away and down. A knife cuts best when being either pulled or pushed in a slightly lateral motion. Never cut straight down perpendicularly as this results in uneven cuts.

Peeling

When peeling root vegetables and tubers, turn the knife on its side and use the base. Hold the vegetable firmly in the left hand and lay the knife along the surface of the vegetable and your thumb over the peel to gauge its thickness and the depth of the cut. Place your index finger on top of the back of the blade to push the knife along.

Chopping

Begin chopping parsley and the like by cutting the vegetable roughly using the pushing technique. Then hold the tip of the knife down on the board with your left hand while working the rest of the blade up and down in a lever motion with your right hand. Rotate it left and right to chop evenly. This is the quickest way to chop finely.

Care and Cleaning of Knives

Knives need to be clean and sharp to work well. After each use, wash the knife immediately and wipe dry. At the end of the day, polish according to the following instructions. Lay the knife flat on its side on a cutting board. Hold it firmly to avoid accidents. Sprinkle some cleanser on the flat end of a piece of carrot or cucumber, or a cabbage stem, and use it to polish both sides of the blade. (A wine bottle cork—soaked in water to remove the wine—can be used instead of a vegetable scrubber.) Wash the knife, rinse thoroughly with very hot water, and wipe it dry.

Care and Cleaning of Cutting Boards

Cutting boards are generally either wooden or hard plastic. In either case, keeping the board clean is very important. After using, rinse and scour thoroughly with cleanser and a scrub brush. Wipe completely dry. Ideally, at least once a month cutting boards should be sterilized in boiling water and dried in the sun.

Basic Vegetable Cutting Techniques

It is important to choose the right cutting method for any given vegetable. The results must, of course, be attractive, but you should also consider whether the cutting will promote the blending of flavors without damaging the natural texture of the vegetable. The following section introduces the most basic cutting and chopping techniques used in Japanese cooking.

Rounds

Carrots, cucumbers, daikon radishes, and other cylindrical or round vegetables are often cut in equally thick slices to form rounds. The thickness of such rounds should be determined by use.

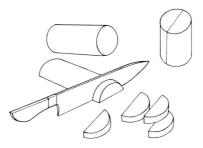

Half-Moons

Cylindrical vegetables are sliced in half lengthwise, then sliced evenly to form half-moon pieces. Again, the thickness of each piece will depend on how it is to be used.

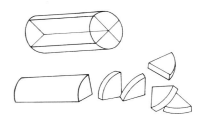

Quarter-Rounds (Ginkgo Leaf Cut)

This method produces quarter-rounds which resemble the leaves of the ginkgo tree. Again, this is generally used with cylindrical vegetables like carrots, daikon radishes, and so on. Quarter the vegetable lengthwise and cut each quarter in even slices. Adjust thickness according to use.

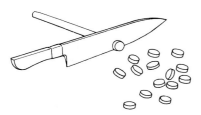

Edge Cut

For narrow cylindrical ingredients like green onions, this technique involves simply shaving thin slices from the end of the vegetable. Adjust the thickness of the slice depending on the vegetable. This cut produces extremely thin rounds.

Diagonal Cut

This technique is also for cylindrical vegetables. Cut evenly thick slices on the diagonal.

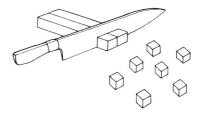

Cube Cut

To make ⅜-inch (1-cm) cubes, simply cut the bars in the last technique in ⅜-inch (1-cm) lengths.

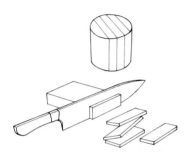

Rectangular Cut

Cut the vegetable (carrot, daikon radish, and so on) in 1½–2-inch (4–5-cm) lengths and slice lengthwise in ⅜-inch (1-cm) wide pieces. Lay each slice flat and slice thinly lengthwise.

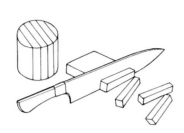

Bar Cut

For daikon radish and similar vegetables, begin by cutting in 1½–2-inch (4–5-cm) lengths, then slice these lengthwise in ⅜-inch (1-cm) thick pieces. Cut these pieces again in ⅜-inch (1-cm) wide strips.

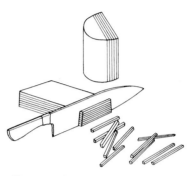

Julienne Cut

First cut in 1½–2-inch (4–5-cm) lengths. Cut these lengthwise in thin slices, stack the slices, and cut them again lengthwise to form matchstick pieces.

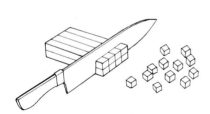

Dice Cut

Follow the instructions for cube cut but reduce the size of the cubes to about ¼ inch (5 mm).

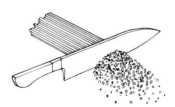

Fine Chopping

Julienned pieces are chopped into fine pieces, then chopped again (see p. 27).

Wedge Cut

Use this technique for round or oval fruits and vegetables—tomatoes, lemons, and so on. Cut in half and then slice from the center into wedges.

Preparing Vegetables

How to Boil Spinach

Depending on whether spinach is boiled or steamed, the strength of its smell and amount of water retained will differ. In Japanese cooking, spinach is generally cooked in ample boiling water just until its color changes. Although steaming spinach is better from a nutritional standpoint, the characteristic harsh smell that remains does not go well with the delicate and subtle flavors of Japanese cooking. In this book, spinach is cooked in lightly salted, ample boiling water.

Wash the spinach in a large bowl filled with cool water. Dirt tends to cling to the backs of leaves and the roots so wash these parts carefully. If the spinach roots are large, make two perpendicular cuts in their tips to allow them to cook properly.

In a large saucepan, boil ample, lightly salted water (1 tsp of salt to 4 cups/1 liter of water). Insert the spinach, root end first, into the boiling water. Strike the root end against the bottom of the saucepan several times before immersing the spinach completely. This loosens any dirt that might remain on the roots.

Do not overcook the spinach. When the color changes to a bright green and the spinach is cooked through, remove and place in cold water for 1–2 minutes. Drain in a colander. Squeeze out excess water with your hands or a bamboo rolling mat. Lay the spinach in the mat, somewhat closer to you than center, alternating the end the roots fall on. Roll the mat up and squeeze gently.

Swiss chard, red chard, kale, Chinese cabbage, and cabbage are boiled in the same way and drained in a colander.

Rather than immersing the spinach in water to cool and to preserve its bright green color, boiled spinach can be drained in a colander and fanned until cool. Water-cooled spinach absorbs excess water which must be thoroughly squeezed out before using.

How to Boil Green Beans, Snow Peas, and Green Soybeans

These three vegetables are washed, rubbed with salt, then added to ample boiling water and cooked. This method brings out the beautiful green of the pods. After boiling, place in a colander to drain, and fan to cool. Rapid cooling prevents the bright green from fading.

The pods of green soybeans are covered with little hairs which are removed by rubbing with the salt. Before boiling, cut both ends of the pod with a scissors so the beans will become soft and the salt can penetrate to the beans. When using frozen green soybeans, do not defrost. Place the frozen green soybeans directly in the boiling water.

Green soybeans are usually boiled before eating, but green beans and snow peas are softer and can be lightly steamed instead of boiled. To steam, rub the green beans and snow peas with salt, steam, then fan until cool.

How to Boil Other Vegetables

Asparagus

Break off the tough ends of the stems near the roots and peel the lower part of the stems. Bring ample, lightly salted water (1 tsp to 4 cups/1 liter of water) to a boil. Insert the asparagus stems first, then the tips. Boil until tender. Drain in a colander and fan to cool. Asparagus can be steamed if desired.

Okra

Wash the okra and rub it with salt. Place in boiling water and cook until the okra changes color. Be careful not to overcook. Drain in a colander and fan to cool. Okra can also be steamed.

Trefoil (*Mitsuba*)

Wash the trefoil and cut off the roots. Submerge briefly in boiling water, then drain in a colander. Fan to cool.

Bean Sprouts

Place the bean sprouts in a large bowl filled with water and wash, changing the water several times. Bring ample water to a boil and add some rice vinegar (1 Tbsp of rice vinegar to 4 cups/1 liter of water). Add the bean sprouts and boil until tender but still firm. Drain in a colander and cool.

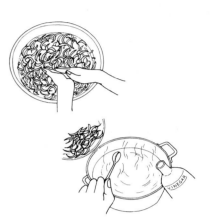

Ridding Vegetables of Their Harshness

Some vegetables have a unique acrid harshness that can cause discoloration when cooked. While it is not necessary to remove the responsible elements from a health standpoint, Japanese cooking emphasizes the presentation of food and delicate flavors so these elements are usually removed or prevented from having an effect.

Lotus Root (*Renkon*)

Wash and peel the lotus root. Cut as directed in the recipe and immediately immerse in vinegared water (1 Tbsp of rice vinegar for every cup of water). To cook, put a little rice vinegar in ample boiling water and then add the lotus root. The vinegar prevents discoloration. If lotus root is not peeled before boiling, the skin turns a purplish black, and if other vegetables are being boiled at the same time, the boiling liquid turns murky. If you want to use lotus root without peeling it, fry it in a little sesame oil before boiling with other vegetables.

Burdock Root (*Gobo*)

Wash and scrub with a vegetable brush to remove the skin. After cutting as directed in the recipe, immediately place in vinegared water (1 Tbsp rice vinegar to every cup water) to keep the burdock from discoloring. Bring ample water to a boil, add a little rice vinegar to the water, then add the burdock root. To prevent discoloration when using unpeeled burdock root, first fry it well in sesame oil before boiling it with other vegetables.

Mountain Yam (*Yamaimo*)

Mountain yam is often eaten raw, but it discolors after being cut. After peeling, immediately immerse in vinegared water (1 Tbsp rice vinegar to every cup of water). Remove from the water and wipe dry with a clean towel. Grate or chop. To prevent discoloration, sprinkle a little rice vinegar on top or mix it in.

Restoring Seaweed

In Japan, seaweed has long been an important part of the daily diet and an essential ingredient in many traditional dishes. Nutritious, low-calorie, and delicious, seaweed—particularly *nori*—is gaining popularity in the United States.

Wakame Seaweed

When trying to determine how much dried *wakame* to use, remember that when *wakame* is restored, it expands to 7–8 times its dry volume.

1. Wash the dirt and sand from the *wakame* and soak it for 4–5 minutes in a bowl with water to cover.

2. If the *wakame* is to be used in a salad, pour boiling water over it. If the *wakame* is still not soft enough, immerse it briefly in boiling water and remove with a slotted spoon.

3. Cut the tough vein off, and cut in bite-sized pieces.

Hijiki Seaweed

When estimating how much dried *hijiki* seaweed to use, remember that restored *hijiki* expands to 4–5 times its original size.

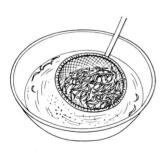

1. Wash the *hijiki* seaweed by placing it in a bowl filled with water and stirring with your hands to loosen the dirt. Scoop up the *hijiki* with a slotted spoon and transfer to another bowl filled with water. Soak for 5–10 minutes.

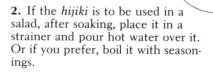

2. If the *hijiki* is to be used in a salad, after soaking, place it in a strainer and pour hot water over it. Or if you prefer, boil it with seasonings.

Wakame Seaweed

Wakame is a fringed, dark green, nutritious seaweed that thrives in strong ocean currents. It is harvested, washed, and sun-dried before marketing. It is delicious in soups and in salads.

Hijiki Seaweed

Hijiki is a very common and popular seaweed that is delicious and refreshing with other vegetables. It is extremely rich in calcium and protein, vitamins A, B, B^{12}, and iron.

Konbu Seaweed

Konbu's unique flavor has made it an essential feature of Japanese cooking. *Konbu* is rich in vitamins and minerals and grows in abundance in oceans around the world. It is sold dried, and the best quality is thick and green with flecks of brownish black. The white powder that coats *konbu* is called mannitol and has a slightly sweet flavor. Do not wash it off in water. Simply wipe excess powder or debris from the seaweed with a dry towel. Placed in a moisture-free, airtight jar, *konbu* will keep up to six months without

Preparing Fish and Shellfish

Getting Clams to Expel Sand and Dirt

Place live short-neck, hard-shell, and other seawater clams in a salt-water brine (1 Tbsp salt for every 4 cups/1 liter water). Let the clams rest in this water undisturbed for half a day or overnight. A few clams may remain closed after soaking. Test each clam by striking it against another clam. A dull sound means the clam has died and should be discarded.

Washing Shelled Clams

Place the shelled clams in a strainer and place them, strainer and all, in a bowl filled with salt-water brine (1 Tbsp salt for every 4 cups/1 liter of water). Shake to wash, making sure to remove any remaining shell fragments. Take the clams and the strainer out of the salt water and wash by running cold water over them. Drain thoroughly.

Preparing Red Shell (*Akagai*)

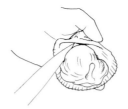

1. Insert your knife in the black ligament that acts as a hinge at the back of the shell and open it, twisting the knife as necessary.

2. With the blade of the knife, cut the flesh away from the shell.

3. Cut away the flesh that surrounds the main part of the meat.

Note:
If red shell is not available at your local fish market, you may be able to get a Japanese restaurant or sushi shop to sell some to you.

4. Insert your knife in the middle of the flesh and cut the flesh of the red shell in half.

5. Cut away the black organs, on the inner side of the red shell flesh.

---

refrigeration. Frozen, it will keep indefinitely. *Konbu* is also roasted and ground to make a naturally saltly tea.

Nori Seaweed

Nori is the most well known of all seaweeds, probably due to the popularity of *nori*-wrapped sushi rolls. *Nori* seaweed is cultivated intensively in the shallow waters along the coasts of Japan. It is harvested, washed carefully, and then pressed dry in thin, square sheets, giving it its distinctive paperlike appearance.

Tosakanori, see pp. 72, 86

Preparing Squid

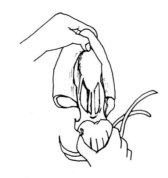

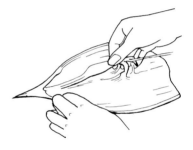

1. Make a cut in the middle of the back of the squid and holding it open with your thumbs, remove the cartilage.

2. Hold the body sac with your left hand and the tentacles with your right. Gently pull the tentacles and the innards away from the body sac.

3. Remove the transparent quill.

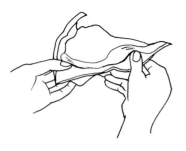

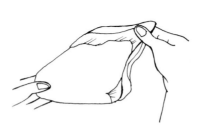

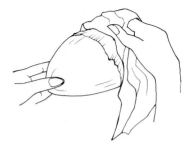

4. Insert your thumb between the skin and the body along the cut and flip it over.

5. Holding the top of the body, peel the skin away.

6. Using a damp, non-terry kitchen towel, rub away the inner skin of the squid.

Washing Shelled Oysters

1. Grate some daikon radish into a bowl. For every 8 oz (200 g) of oysters, use a 1-inch (3-cm) length of daikon radish (2½ oz/70 g).

2. Rinse the oysters in cold water, then place them in the bowl with the grated daikon radish. Stir the mixture with your hand to remove any remaining dirt or fragments of shell.

3. When the grated daikon radish starts to look dirty, transfer the entire contents of the bowl to a strainer and wash in lightly salted water. Wash until all the grated daikon radish is removed, run cold water over the oysters to clean them, and drain.

Filleting by the Three-Part Slicing Method

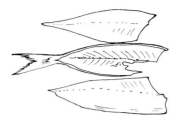 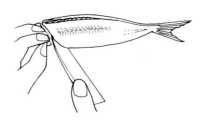 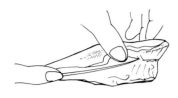

1. This method produces two fillets, one cut from each side of the fish, and the skeleton with a fair amount of flesh on it.

2. To cut off the head, lift the pectoral fin and insert your knife at its base. Cut diagonally behind the gills toward the center of the fish. Repeat from the other side.

3. Slice from the head end to the tail along the belly of the fish and remove the innards with the tip of the knife. Wash the fish with lightly salted water.

4. Slice off a fillet starting from the head end and working toward the tail with your knife along the backbone of the fish. Flip the fish over and repeat.

5. Remove any remaining bones from the belly of the fish with the tip of the knife.

Thinly Sliced Fillets

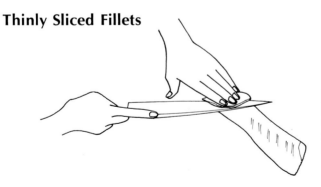
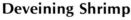

Place the fillet skin side up. With a knife held at an acute angle, cut a very thin slice of fish off, cutting across the grain, from the left of the fillet.

Deveining Shrimp

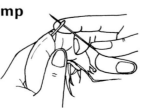

Bend the back of the shrimp slightly at a point between the second and third shell segments from its head. Insert the tip of a bamboo skewer below the vein and gently pull the vein out.

Cooking Rice

The rice salads on pages 14 and 23 are based on the plain short-grain white rice that forms an important part of every Japanese meal. Nutritious brown rice, shown on page 17, is made a little differently than white rice. You may want to experiment with brown rice salads.

The best saucepan for making rice is a thick-walled stainless steel or ceramic pot with a sturdy, well-fitting lid.

Cooking Short-Grain White Rice

Washing the Rice

As the amount of water to be added in cooking depends on how much rice is used, always measure the rice carefully. Wash the rice about 20–30 minutes before cooking.

Place the rice in a bowl filled with water and stir it around with your hand. Remove any dirt. Pour off the water and rub the rice, pushing it toward the back of the bowl with the palm of your hand. Add water again, stir well, then pour off and save the water. This milky water contains nutrients, so it should be saved and used. This water is especially good for boiling root vegetables like daikon radish.

Rub and rinse the rice 2–3 times more, and drain in a colander. Let rest for about 30 minutes. Rubbing and washing the rice should be done very quickly, the whole process taking no longer than 3–4 minutes. White rice is very dry and its surface is covered with powdered bran. Washing and polishing make it easy for the rice to absorb water, and if too much time is spent on the process, the smell of the bran tends to penetrate into the rice grains.

Determining How Much Water Should Be Used

There are two ways to determine how much water should be used. One way is to measure the washed rice that has been let stand for about 30 minutes. The rice will have absorbed water and be about 1.2 times its original volume. Transfer the washed rice to a saucepan and add an equal amount of water.

Or transfer the rice immediately after washing to a saucepan and add 1.2 parts water to 1 part of rice (measured when dry). Let stand in the pot for 20–30 minutes before cooking.

The amount of water to be used also depends on the type of rice and how fresh it is. Short-grain white rice that was harvested within the last six months contains a lot of moisture and the added water should be reduced to 1.1 times the amount of rice. More mature rice and partly polished rice (with the rice germ still intact) require 1.2 parts of water to 1 part rice. Long-grain white rice and brown rice require 1.3–1.5 parts water to 1 part rice.

Cooking the Rice

Put the lid on the pot. Bring the water to a boil over high heat for a large quantity (5 cups) and over medium high for a small quantity (3 cups). When the water comes to a boil, lower the heat to medium and cook for 5–6 minutes for a large quantity and 3–4 minutes for a small quantity, making sure the pot does not boil over. On low heat, cook for another 12–13 minutes for a large quantity and 15 minutes for a small quantity of rice. Cook very briefly, about 10 seconds, on high, then remove from heat. Let the cooked rice stand in the pot for about 15 minutes to let the heat of the rice and the pot complete the cooking process.

After Cooking the Rice

Transfer the cooked rice to a wooden tub or large wooden salad bowl, cover with a non-terry kitchen towel, and place a lid over the towel. If using a Japanese wooden tub, first wipe it with a damp towel to prevent sticking. Rice paddles also should be moistened before use.

If the rice is left in the pot, the steam from the rice will turn to water, fall on the rice, and make it sticky. It will cool and harden in the shape of the pot, losing its flavor. So after the rice has stood for 15 minutes, use a rice paddle with a sideways, cutting motion to fluff the rice. Transfer it to a wooden tub or salad bowl, and fluff a little more. The wooden tub lets excess moisture escape, preserving the rice's fluffiness. If you do not have a wooden tub or salad bowl, use a rice paddle in the same way to fluff the rice in the pot, cover with a towel, and replace the lid.

If using a rice cooker, follow the manufacturer's directions.

Cooking Brown Rice

Using a Pressure Cooker

Measure the brown rice (1 cup rice makes 2–3 servings). Just before cooking, rinse the rice, changing the water 1–2 times. There is no need to rub brown rice with your hands as you must with white rice. When brown rice is washed, the water will not turn a cloudy white, and there is no need to worry about losing nutrients.

Drain the rice in a colander. Place the rice in a pressure cooker and add water (1.3 parts water to 1 part rice). Add a pinch of salt, attach the lid and tighten the knob (this feature differs depending on the manufacturer). Place over high heat.

After the pressure cooker starts to hiss and the knob begins to revolve, cook for 2 minutes, then reduce the heat to low and cook for 25 minutes. (Depending on the type of pressure cooker, this can be as much as 40–45 minutes. Follow the manufacturer's directions.)

Remove from heat and let stand for 15 minutes. Remove the knob. After making sure that the steam has escaped, remove the lid and use a rice paddle to fluff the rice with a cutting motion.

If you prefer softer brown rice, wash the rice and soak it in water for several hours before cooking. When boiling the rice, use 1.3 times as much water as rice.

Using a Metal Pot

Wash the rice and soak it for a few hours before cooking. Measure the rice before washing it and use 1.4–1.5 parts water to 1 part rice. Place the pot over medium heat. When the water comes to a boil, increase the heat to high and cook for 5 minutes. Reduce the heat to low and cook for 40 minutes more. Remove from heat and let stand for 15 minutes.

Using a Ceramic Pot

Nutritionwise, cooking brown rice over a long period in a ceramic pot is preferable to using a pressure cooker. Flavorwise, a ceramic pot brings out the sweetness of the rice more than an metal pot.

About 6–7 hours before cooking, measure the rice, wash it, and soak it in water (1.5 parts water to each part rice). Place the pot over medium-low heat. When the water boils, reduce the heat to the lowest setting or flame possible and cook for 40 minutes. Remove from heat and let stand for 15 minutes.

Dashi

This mild but fragrant soup stock, made from *konbu* seaweed and bonito flakes and known as *dashi*, is an important ingredient in many dressings and traditional Japanese dishes. *Dashi* made from *konbu* alone is also quite common. *Dashi* is used for soups and boiled dishes in addition to dressings and sauces.

Konbu Dashi

Wipe the *konbu* on both sides with a dry cloth. Make 2–3 deep cuts in the *konbu* perpendicular to the veins, place in the water, and let stand overnight. Remove *konbu* before using.

Makes 2½ cups (600 ml) *dashi*

2½ cups (600 ml) water
4 × 6-inch (10 × 15-cm) piece *konbu* seaweed (⅓ oz/10 g)

Regular *Dashi*

1. Wipe the *konbu* with a dry cloth and make 2–3 cuts perpendicular to the veins. Place the water in a saucepan, add the *konbu*, and place over medium heat for 5–6 minutes.

2. Just before the water reaches a boil, remove the *konbu*. Stock in which *konbu* has been allowed to boil becomes murky and develops an unpleasant odor.

Makes 2½ cups (600 ml) *dashi*

3 cups (700 ml) water
4 × 6-inch (10 × 15-cm) piece *konbu* seaweed (⅓ oz/10 g)
⅔ cup bonito flakes (¼ oz/8 g)

3. When the water boils, add the bonito flakes, boil only about 10 seconds, and remove from heat.

4. Immediately skim any foam off the surface, and then let stand 3 minutes while the bonito flakes settle to the bottom.

Freezing *Dashi*

As most dressing recipes call for just a small amount of *dashi*, you may find it easier to make a large batch and freeze it in ice trays. Frozen, *dashi* will keep almost indefinitely. Premeasure the amount of *dashi* in each cube and then thaw as needed.

Re-using the *Konbu*

Save the *konbu* used in making *dashi*. Slice it in thin strips and place in a saucepan. Add 3 Tbsps of water, 3 Tbsps of saké, and ½ tsp rice vinegar. Place over medium heat. When the *konbu* softens, add 1 tsp soy sauce and ½ tsp *mirin*, and continue simmering until the liquid is completely evaporated. The *konbu* then may be eaten by itself or combined with a mild-flavored vegetable for a tasty salad.

5. Place a colander over a bowl, line it with cheesecloth (or a non-terry kitchen towel), and pour the stock through. Do not squeeze the excess liquid from the cloth.

6. This method produces the best *dashi*. If you need to store it, add a pinch of salt and refrigerate. It will keep 1–2 days.

Re-using the Bonito Flakes

After making *dashi*, transfer the bonito flakes to a frying pan and heat, stirring constantly, on high until they are dry. Add 1 tsp parched sesame seeds and a pinch of salt and blend well. This mixture makes a good topping for salads or pasta.

Basic Seasonings

A broad range of effects can be achieved with dressings based on vinegar, soy sauce, and miso. When the seasonings being added are strong, however, it is also common to use *dashi* (bonito and *konbu* seaweed stock) to give the dressing a milder flavor.

Vinegar

In Japan, the most commonly used vinegar is rice vinegar, but a variety of other vinegars are in fact produced and used on occasion. There is a brown rice version (*genmaisu*) of the standard rice vinegar, and other grain vinegars include barley and rye. There are also fruit vinegars made from the juice of a small, sour citron (*ponzu*) or plum (*umezu*). The vinegar used in this book is rice vinegar (or brown rice vinegar), but you may try substituting any grain vinegar, cider vinegar, wine vinegar, and so on, keeping in mind the taste differences.

Ponzu can be used in the Daikon-Vinegar Dressing (p. 50), or the Cucumber-Daikon Dressing (p. 51). *Umezu* can be used in the Pickled Plum Dressing (p. 52). Either of these two vinegars is good in the Vinegar-Soy Dressing (p. 56).

Soy Sauce

There are two basic kinds of soy sauce: dark and light. Dark soy sauce is deep brown and has a strong flavor. Light soy sauce is thinner and slightly saltier. In this book, recipes calling for "soy sauce" refer to the dark variety. Light soy sauce is referred to as such. If you only keep one bottle on hand, the dark is recommended. When substituting dark for light, reduce the amount slightly and adjust the salt.

Bonito Flakes

This basic Japanese seasoning begins with large fillets of fresh bonito. They are steamed and then dried until they become as hard as wood. You can buy these hard blocks and shave off flakes as needed or you can buy preshaven, packaged bonito flakes. They are often sold as "Kezuri bushi" or "hana katsuo." When buying bonito flakes look for ones that are translucent. Avoid flakes that have been crushed in tiny pieces or that appear murky or opaque. Store them in a jar and keep them dry. They will keep up to 3 months.

Mirin

Mirin, a thick cooking saké, adds sweetness and flavor to a variety of dressings. It is, however, 14 percent alcohol, so for recipes using large amounts of *mirin* it is best to remove the alcohol. This can be done either by lighting the *mirin* with a match and letting the alcohol burn off or heating over low heat to a boil. Most of the recipes in this book, however, call for only small amounts of *mirin*, so such steps are unnecessary. If you do not have *mirin* on hand, substitute 1 Tbsp saké mixed with 1 tsp of brown sugar for each tablespoon *mirin*.

Miso

Miso, fermented soybean paste, is one of the most important elements of the Japanese diet. It is used in making condiments and soups and as a seasoning for dressings and many traditional dishes. Basically, soybeans, salt, and grain are fermented with a special rice mold culture called *koji-kin*. The presence of this culture makes miso beneficial to digestion. There are three main types of miso, *mugi* (barley) miso, *kome* (rice) miso, and *mame* (grainless) miso. *Mugi* miso and *kome* miso are the more popular types and consumed almost daily in the average Japanese household. Miso can also be classified by color, red or white.

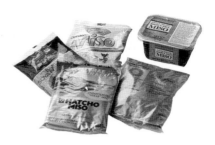

Mugi miso is a red miso, actually dark brown in color. To make *mugi* miso, first barley is cooked, cooled down to the proper temperature, and mixed with the rice mold. It is let stand for two or three days and turns a greenish yellow as the culture grows, forming barley *koji*. Next, soybeans are cooked until tender, mashed, cooled, and mixed with the barley *koji*. Salt is added and the mixture stirred well. The miso is edible after half a year, during which temperature and texture are carefully monitored to encourage the growth of the culture. However, miso is best after fermenting at least two years, enough time for the flavors to become rich and deep. Red miso will keep up to six months if refrigerated.

Kome miso is made in the same way except rice *koji* is used in place of the barley *koji*. *Kome* miso can be either red or white and ranges from dark brown to a pale yellow in color and salty to sweet in taste. Shinshu miso is a mild, non-sweet, yellowish brown type of *kome* miso. The sweetest, lightest colored version of *kome* miso is white miso, sometimes called Saikyo miso. The fermentation time for white miso is short, a few weeks after the rice *koji* and soybeans are mixed. White miso is especially delicious in salad dressings and soups and is used for most of the recipes in this book. Since white miso has a lower salt content than red, it should be kept refrigerated and used within six months.

Mame miso uses only beans, no grain. Usually it is made from soybeans, but it can be made from black beans or some other kind of bean, although grain is never added. *Mame* miso is dark, rich, and chunky red miso, best for soup. The most popular *mame* miso is Hatcho miso, named after its place of origin in Okazaki, Aichi Prefecture. The best Hatcho miso is allowed to mature for three to five years.

When purchasing miso, make sure that the culture is still active or many of its health benefits will be lost. Check to be sure it has not been pasteurized and contains no preservatives. Miso made from whole grains, brown rice, or whole grain barley will have the best flavor, aroma, and texture.

Sesame Seeds

Sesame seeds are an essential part of many traditional Japanese dishes and are the major ingredient in *goma-ae* salads, literally "sesame-dressed" salads. Sesame seeds contain calcium, phosphorus, and linoleic acid, and are thought to prevent hardening of the arteries. Sesame seeds are parched, ground to a paste, flavored, and used to dress vegetables. Their rich, nutty taste and fragrant aroma make them a very pleasant way to add nutrition to a salad. Parched sesame seeds, both black and white, can be used whole, lightly crushed, partially ground, or ground to a paste.

Goma-shio (sesame salt) is a mixture of black sesame seeds and sea salt. It is reputed to be a cure for heartburn and seasickness. Use a small amount as a topping on cooked rice and other grains. To make sesame salt, use 15 parts roasted sesame seeds to 1 part roasted fine sea salt. Mix and grind in a *suribachi* or mortar until well crushed. The sesame should thoroughly coat the sea salt. Keep in an airtight jar.

Sesame Oil

Sesame oil, a potent, aromatic pressing from sesame seeds, is a delicious addition to salad dressings. It comes in light and dark brown varieties. The light sesame oil has a correspondingly light aroma and taste. Dark sesame oil is made from parched sesame seeds and its color and flavor reflect the parching, being darker and heavier. It should be added sparingly.

Sesame oil, like the seeds themselves, is rich in vitamin E. It is also high in fatty acids, which help remove cholesterol from the blood, so use it not only in fried dishes, but in salads as well.

Pickled Plums (*Umeboshi*)

The naturally pickled *umeboshi* is a tart, round, red pickle. Pickled 'plum' is actually a misnomer as the fruit is really a relative of the apricot. At one time, it was an essential part of the daily diet in Japan although consumption has declined somewhat. The pickled plum stimulates the appetite and aids in digestion by keeping the intestinal tract clear. It is also helpful in maintaining an alkaline blood quality.

Plum trees bear delicate, fragrant white blossoms in the depth of winter. The fruit is picked in June, before it ripens and when its beneficial citric acid content is at its peak. The small juicy plums, still green, are pickled for a month in sea salt with red *shiso* leaves added to impart color. Then for at least a week, the plums are spread out on rice-straw mats to dry in the sun. It is this process which gives the pickled plums their wrinkled appearance and also their name in Japanese (literally, dried plums). Then, the plums are returned to their kegs and left to age in their own juice for up to one year, after which they can be kept indefinitely.

Pickled plum vinegar (*ume-zu*) is a deliciously tart, vivid red juice drawn from the pickled plums. Both pickled plum vinegar and brown rice vinegar are considered to be high quality, gourmet vinegars. Use pickled plum vinegar in sauces, spreads, dips, and dressings to add a mildly sour taste.

Pickled plum paste (sold as "red umeboshi paste") is available in most Asian markets and natural food stores, but it is often mixed with red *shiso* leaves. A good paste can easily be made (see p. 52) from natural pickled plums like those shown here, which have been pickled for up to a year by the traditional process.

Salt

Unrefined sea salt tends to have a mellower flavor than the widely used refined variety.

Sugar

The rules of Japanese cooking (as with much else in Japanese culture) revolve around fives. A balanced meal must combine the Five Flavors (sweet, hot, salty, bitter, and sour), Five Colors (red, yellow, green, white, and black), and Five Methods (raw, grilled, steamed, boiled, and fried). Depending on the meal, the role of the sweet element occasionally falls to the salad—thus, logically, one needs salads that are sweet. In the interest of preserving traditional flavors, some of the recipes in this book use sugar—but brown sugar, never refined white sugar.

Equipment

Suribachi (Japanese Mortar)

The *suribachi* is a ceramic mortar with a grooved interior. Its pestle is made of wood. Hold one end of the pestle in the cupped palm of your left hand and keep it stationary. Grip the middle of the pestle with your right hand and rotate the pestle, pressing down. A *suribachi* may tend to move about on the counter as you grind; try putting a slightly damp towel underneath to prevent slipping. After use, scour the *suribachi* with a brush and cleanser, paying special attention to the grooves. Wipe it dry and store in a dry place. If you do not have a Japanese *suribachi*, a standard Western mortar—preferably ceramic—may be used instead.

Fine Drum Sieve (*Uragoshi*)

The most common sieve in Japan is a round wooden frame strung with a fine net of horse hair. When using, first dampen the net and tap off excess water. Wet a kitchen towel, wring it out thoroughly, and spread it on the working surface. Place a bowl large enough to hold the sieve on the towel and set the sieve on the bowl with the net side up. Turn the sieve so the openings in the net appear as diamond shapes. The hair should run obliquely, not parallel and perpendicular to you. Force solid food through the net with a flat wooden rice paddle. After use, wash the net under running water with a cloth. Scrub the frame with a brush and dry well before storing. Fine metal sieves can be used if you do not have a Japanese-style fine drum sieve.

Graters

Graters are made of copper, aluminum, plastic, and various other materials, but from the point of view of strength and sharpness, copper graters are superior. The standard grater has spikes for coarse grating on one side and spikes for finer grating on the reverse. Select the side appropriate for your vegetable and recipe. After using a metal grater, let it soak in water to loosen the vegetable fibers, then rinse and dry thoroughly before storing.

Bamboo Rolling Mats (*Makisu*)

These flexible mats are made of strips of bamboo woven together with cotton string. They are often used for rolling sushi, but they are also very convenient for squeezing excess liquid from vegetables. The photograph shows one being used on spinach. The trick is to apply pressure evenly to avoid damaging the vegetable. The bamboo rolling mat can also be spread over a bowl and used to drain grated daikon, tofu, and so on. After using, wash and dry thoroughly before storing.

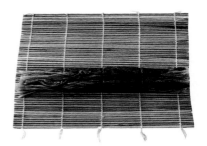

BASIC DRESSINGS

Ohitashi Dressing

This dressing is the starting point for the simplest and most frequently encountered vegetable dishes in Japan. *Ohitashi* dressing is essentially no more than a modified soy sauce marinade. The seasoning is mild so it adapts well to a number of vegetables.

1 cup (240 ml) *dashi*
2 Tbsps *mirin*
2 Tbsps light soy sauce

1. Place the *dashi* in a shallow pan, add the *mirin* and light soy sauce, and mix well.

2. Spread the salad ingredients out to allow the dressing to penetrate. Soak for 10 minutes.

3. Drain or squeeze to remove excess Dressing.

Spinach with *Ohitashi* Dressing

Make two cuts into the tip of the spinach roots at right angles to each other (see p. 30). Wash the leaves thoroughly. Add the spinach to ample lightly salted boiling water and boil until tender. Drain, then rinse in cold water, drain again. Cut off the roots. Lay the spinach lengthwise on a bamboo rolling mat. Wrap the mat around the spinach and squeeze out the excess water.

Prepare the *Ohitashi* Dressing as directed above.

Add the boiled spinach to the Dressing and spread it out to allow even absorption. Let it stand for about 10 minutes. Drain and squeeze out excess liquid using the bamboo rolling mat.

Cut the spinach leaves into 1–1½-inch (3–4-cm) lengths and partially separate the bundles.

Mound the dressed spinach in individual dishes and garnish the top with some bonito flakes before serving.

Serves 4
42 calories

10 oz (300 g) spinach
pinch salt
Ohitashi Dressing
2 Tbsps bonito flakes

VARIATIONS AND NOTES

The *mirin* can be deleted if you prefer a slightly less sweet dressing. This dressing is good with chrysanthemum leaves, bean sprouts, cabbage, Chinese cabbage, trefoil, eggplant, and so on. It can also be used with Japanese mushrooms such as *shimeji* and *enoki*.

Sesame Seed Dressing

Parched sesame seeds are ground and seasoned with soy sauce, *mirin*, and *dashi* for one of the most popular Japanese dressings. The richness of sesame complements less highly flavored vegetables. Serve as a side dish with bland main dishes, use as an appetizer, or use the dressing as a dip for raw vegetables.

5 Tbsps white sesame seeds
1 tsp *mirin*
1 tsp light soy sauce
2 Tbsps *dashi* (or water)

1. Place the sesame seeds in a dry, heavy saucepan or frying pan and parch them over low heat, shaking the pan constantly, until the aroma is released and a few seeds begin to jump out of the pan. Remove from heat.

2. Dampen a non-terry kitchen towel and lightly wring it out. Place a clean, dry *suribachi* on the towel, add the hot, parched sesame seeds, and grind them. Note that the seeds in the photograph are **partially ground**.

3. As you continue grinding, sesame oil will be released and the seeds will form a sticky paste.

4. Scrape the grooves of the *suribachi* with a bamboo skewer and gather the paste in the center. Add the *mirin*, soy sauce, and *dashi* and mix well.

5. Use the Dressing as it is, or if you prefer a smoother consistency, force the mixture through a fine sieve.

6. Mix the Dressing with cut salad vegetables and toss.

Cucumber with Sesame Seed Dressing

Slice the cucumbers in very thin rounds. Place them in a bowl and sprinkle with salt. Let stand 1–2 minutes until the rounds become somewhat soft, then use your hands to squeeze out some of the excess moisture.

Prepare the Sesame Seed Dressing as directed above.

Just before serving, add the cucumbers to the Dressing and mix gently until the cucumbers are well coated. Avoid damaging the cucumbers by stirring too vigorously. Arrange in individual dishes.

VARIATIONS AND NOTES

This dressing can also be made with prepared sesame paste. Brown sugar may be substituted for the *mirin*, or leave the sweetener out altogether if you prefer.

Sesame Seed Dressing suits a wide variety of vegetables: most leafy greens, cabbage, Chinese cabbage, bean sprouts, eggplant, snow peas, lotus root, burdock root, and so on.

Serves 4

78 calories

3 Japanese cucumbers
(10 oz/300 g)
½ tsp salt
Sesame Seed Dressing

Chopped Sesame Dressing

Parch the black sesame to release its wonderful aroma and flavor, then chop it coarsely—that's all there is to this simply delicious dressing. Sesame seeds are rich in vitamin B^1 and iron, but the tough hulls make it difficult for the body to absorb this goodness. They also prevent the flavor from being fully appreciated. Thus, most recipes call for sesame seeds to be chopped, pounded, crushed, or ground. Use whichever way seems best to you.

4 Tbsps black sesame seeds

1. Place the sesame seeds in a heavy saucepan and parch them over low heat while shaking the pan back and forth.

2. Lay a dry, non-terry kitchen towel on a cutting board and spread the sesame seeds on it in an even layer. Using a large kitchen knife, coarsely chop the seeds. Or use one of the methods below. Chopping on the cloth prevents the seeds from scattering.

3. Sprinkle the salad ingredients with the chopped sesame and mix gently.

To pound sesame seeds, place the parched seeds on a dry, non-terry kitchen towel, gather the corners to form a pouch, and pound lightly with a wooden pestle.

To crush sesame seeds, knead the parched seeds with your fingertips.

To grind sesame seeds, place the parched seeds in the chamber of a sesame seed mill and turn the handle.

Radishes with Chopped Sesame Dressing

Remove the stems of the radishes and slice them very thinly, lengthwise, with the grain. Sprinkle with salt and place them in a bowl. Weight the radishes with a plate and let stand briefly until they become slightly soft and flexible.

Prepare Chopped Sesame Dressing as directed above.

Just before serving, gently squeeze excess water from the radishes and mix them with the chopped sesame. Arrange in serving dishes.

Serves 4

68 calories

10 oz (300 g) red radishes
1 scant tsp salt
Chopped Sesame Dressing

VARIATIONS AND NOTES

In general, there are two types of sesame seeds—black and white. They may be used interchangeably in this recipe. Select the color to match or complement the vegetable you are serving or even the dish you are serving it in. With black sesame try daikon radishes, turnips, onions, or potatoes (parboiled and julienne cut). Leafy greens, green vegetables, corn and the like go well with white sesame.

Tofu Dressing

Partially dried tofu is the basis for this typical mixture of sesame paste, brown sugar, soy sauce, and salt. Traditionally, this dressing uses very little or no salt and is somewhat sweet, but the seasoning can be easily adjusted to blend with the other dishes you are serving. This dressing is delicious in itself, so try increasing the amount of dressing to equal the amount of vegetables. Vegetables dressed in this manner are most attractive when served in small portions on individual serving dishes.

⅔ block regular ("cotton") tofu
(½ lb/200 g)

3 Tbsps white sesame seeds

½ Tbsp brown sugar

dash soy sauce

pinch salt

1. Crumble the tofu and drop it in boiling water to cover. While breaking the tofu into still smaller pieces, continue boiling until the tofu rises to the surface.

2. Line a colander with a non-terry kitchen towel or cheesecloth and add the tofu. Fold the edges of the cloth over the tofu and set a plate or other light weight on top. Let stand 5 minutes to drain thoroughly.

3. Place the parched sesame seeds in a dry *suribachi* and grind to a fine paste (see p. 44).

4. Add the tofu and continue to grind until well incorporated. Season with the brown sugar, soy sauce, and salt and blend well.

5. The Dressing can be used at this point or force it through a fine sieve if a smoother consistency is desired.

6. Add the salad ingredients to the Dressing and toss.

Asparagus with Tofu Dressing

Use your fingers to crack the stem ends of the asparagus and peel off the tough outer skin. Cut into ¾-inch (2-cm) lengths.

Bring ample lightly salted water to a boil over high heat. Add the tougher end pieces of asparagus first. When they have boiled briefly, add the rest and continue cooking until just tender. Drain the asparagus and sprinkle lightly with salt. Let stand in a colander until cool.

Prepare the Tofu Dressing as directed above.

Just before serving, combine the asparagus and Dressing and arrange in dishes.

Serves 4

98 calories

15 spears asparagus
(10 oz/300 g)

pinch salt

Tofu Dressing

VARIATIONS AND NOTES

Vegetables with subtle flavors such as carrots, sweet potatoes, leafy greens, and certain types of mushrooms go well with Tofu Dressing. Another good choice is no-calorie *hijiki* seaweed.

Remember that tofu does not keep well. This dressing should be made the same day the tofu is purchased. Refrigerated, it will keep for two or three days.

Okara Dressing

Okara, also known as *unohana*, is seasoned with *mirin* and brown sugar. Egg yolks are added for a brightly colored, tasty dressing, and rice vinegar is added for the finishing touch. *Okara* is a by-product of the tofu-making process—similar to lees. It has gained popularity because it is extremely high in fiber.

1¾ oz (50 g) *okara*
2 tsps *mirin*
1 tsp brown sugar
pinch salt
1 egg yolk
½ Tbsp rice vinegar

1. Rinse the *okara* briefly in cold water, wrap in a clean, dry, non-terry kitchen towel and squeeze out excess moisture. Place the *okara* in a saucepan and stir in the *mirin*, brown sugar, and salt.

2. Place the pan over medium heat and stir until the mixture becomes crumbly and somewhat dry.

3. Mix the egg yolk in well, crumbling the mixture. Add the rice vinegar and blend quickly while continuing to heat. When the mixture is moist, remove from heat.

4. Spread in a thin layer in a shallow pan and let cool to room temperature.

5. Avoid combining the Dressing with raw fish before it is thoroughly cooled since the heat can actually cause the fish to spoil. Just before serving, coat the salad ingredients with the Dressing.

Horse Mackerel with *Okara* Dressing

Sprinkle both sides of each horse mackerel fillet with salt and arrange, skin side down, in a shallow pan. Let stand for 30 minutes.

Cut away the rest of the rib bones and pull out any remaining bones with your fingers, being careful not to damage the flesh.

Clean the surface of the fish with 1 Tbsp rice vinegar and then arrange, skin side down, in the shallow pan. Add rice vinegar to cover and let stand 5 minutes until the flesh turns white. Drain.

Prepare the *Okara* Dressing as directed above.

Peel the skin from the fish working from the head end. Slice the fillets on the diagonal into bite-sized pieces. Coat with the Dressing. Make sure the Dressing is completely cooled.

Arrange the fish in serving dishes and garnish with *sansho* sprigs.

Serves 4
129 calories

½ lb (250 g) horse mackerel fillets (see p. 35)
½ tsp salt
rice vinegar
Okara Dressing
4 *sansho* sprigs for garnish

VARIATIONS AND NOTES

Horse mackerel is only one possibility. Try sashimi-quality raw sardines, salmon, squid, and red shell (*akagai*). Briefly cure the seafood in vinegar before dressing. To dress vegetables like carrots, lotus root, and bamboo shoots with *okara*, parboil them first, perhaps adding some soy sauce to the water. This dressing will not keep, so make only as much as you plan to use. However, frozen *okara* will keep up to six months. To freeze *okara*, wash it thoroughly, wring out excess water, and break it into small pieces.

Green Soybean Dressing

This dressing begins with the young beans still in their pods. Soybeans are rich in protein, vitamin B[1], and calcium, and the green beans in the pods contain lots of vitamin C. The beans have a luscious, slightly sweet flavor, and in Japan they are often parboiled, salted, and eaten right out of the pods as a snack. They can also be mashed and seasoned with salt, *mirin*, and *dashi* for a unique dressing.

½ lb (250 g) green soybeans in the pod (if frozen, adjust cooking time)

1 tsp salt

1 Tbsp *mirin*

1 Tbsp *dashi* (or water)

1. Bring an ample amount of salted water to boil in a saucepan. Add the green soybeans in their pods and boil about 15 minutes until the soybeans are soft enough to crush with your fingers. Drain.

2. While the soybeans are still hot, shell them, and remove the thin outer membranes. As the soybeans cool, they become harder and more difficult to mash, so work fairly rapidly.

3. Place the beans in a *suribachi* and mash them to a coarse but even paste.

4. Grind until the paste is smooth.

5. Add the salt, *mirin*, and *dashi* and blend thoroughly.

6. Add the salad ingredients and blend gently.

Sautéed Eggplant with Green Soybean Dressing

Remove the stems of the eggplants. Cut into ¼-inch (5-mm) quarter-rounds (see p. 28).

Heat the oil in a frying pan, add the eggplant, and sauté until tender. Sprinkle with salt. Transfer to paper towels to remove excess oil. Cool.

Prepare the Green Soybean Dressing as directed above.

Add the sautéed eggplant to the Dressing and mix gently but thoroughly. Arrange in serving dishes.

VARIATIONS AND NOTES

Seafood used with Green Soybean Dressing includes squid, sillago, and abalone. Lotus root, carrots, yams, potatoes, fennel, and other vegetables are also good. If you prefer, vegetables can be marinated briefly in vinegar before adding to the dressing.

Serves 4

138 calories

4–5 Japanese eggplants (1 lb/500 g)

2–3 Tbsps vegetable oil

½ tsp salt

Green Soybean Dressing

Peanut Dressing

Peanuts are ground to a paste and flavored with salt and *dashi* for a rich, distinctive dressing that is high in protein, vitamins B[1] and E, and other nutrients. Combined with the right vegetable, peanut dressing can make a very nutritious, well-balanced dish, or served alone it is a delicious dip.

Unroasted peanuts in their shells are best because they retain their rich aroma, but unsalted Spanish peanuts can be substituted. The procedure can be simplified by starting with a natural peanut butter (avoid those with added sugar and salt).

1¾ oz (50 g) unroasted peanuts in their shells
¼ tsp salt
4 Tbsps *dashi*

1. Shell the peanuts and remove their skins.

2. Spread a clean, dry, non-terry kitchen towel on a large cutting board and coarsely chop the peanuts.

3. Transfer the peanuts to a dry *suribachi*, add salt, and grind until smooth.

4. When the peanuts have become pastelike, slowly begin adding the *dashi*, stirring constantly. Continue adding *dashi* until the mixture reaches the consistency of a loose mayonnaise.

5. Stir until smooth. Scrape the dressing from the grooves of the *suribachi* with a bamboo skewer.

6. Add the salad vegetable to the Dressing and blend gently.

Carrots with Peanut Dressing

Cut the carrots in 1½-inch (4-cm) lengths and julienne. Drop them in boiling water very briefly (about 10 seconds), drain, and sprinkle with salt. Allow to cool to room temperature.

Prepare the Peanut Dressing as directed above.

Just before serving, add the carrots to the Dressing and blend gently.

Serves 4
97 calories

3 carrots (10 oz/300 g)
pinch salt
Peanut Dressing

VARIATIONS AND NOTES

Peanut Dressing enhances a variety of vegetables: leafy greens, Chinese cabbage, snow peas, bean sprouts, eggplant, cabbage, celery, okra, and so on. Adding light soy sauce, vinegar, or brown sugar makes a spicier, but equally appealing dressing. If using natural peanut butter, start with about 2 Tbsps—just add salt and *dashi*.

Daikon-Vinegar Dressing

This simple, refreshing mixture combines the distinctive taste of grated daikon radish with seasoned rice vinegar for a delicious dressing. The hot, sharp taste of daikon radish and vinegar's sourness go well with strong-flavored seafood or vegetables. Daikon is a good source of vitamin C and when grated and served with raw fish and seafood, it acts as an aid to digestion. However, once grated the nutrients are rapidly lost, so assemble the dressing just before serving.

4½-inch (12-cm) length daikon radish (10 oz/300 g)

3 Tbsps rice vinegar

1½ Tbsps *dashi* (or water)

½ Tbsp *mirin*

dash light soy sauce

½ tsp salt

1. Peel the daikon radish.

2. Hold the grater at an angle over a shallow pan, rough side up, and grate the daikon in rapid strokes.

3. Transfer the grated daikon to a colander and allow it to drain naturally for a minute or two.

4. In a small bowl, combine the vinegar, *dashi*, *mirin*, light soy sauce, and salt and mix well.

5. Transfer the drained, grated daikon to a bowl, add the seasoned vinegar, and stir gently.

6. Just before serving, add the salad ingredients to the Dressing and mix gently.

Oysters with Daikon-Vinegar Dressing

Wash the oysters briefly under cool running water and place them in a bowl with the grated daikon radish for cleaning. Mix thoroughly to remove debris and the viscous coating on the oysters (see p. 34). Transfer to a colander and rinse with lightly salted water to remove all the daikon. Drain the oysters and sprinkle with the vinegar.

Prepare the Daikon-Vinegar Dressing as directed above.

Drop the trefoil in lightly salted boiling water for a few seconds, drain, and cut in ⅜-inch (1-cm) lengths.

When ready to serve, add the oysters to the Dressing, mix, arrange in individual dishes, and garnish with trefoil stems.

VARIATIONS AND NOTES

When using this dressing with fish—bonito, tuna, smoked salmon, and so on—increase the vinegar slightly for added tanginess. Daikon-Vinegar Dressing is a good accompaniment for small fishes like *chirimen jako* (tiny dried fish), shellfish, and seaweed.

This dressing can also be used with lighter-flavored mushrooms and even fruit. Try apples, persimmons, or kiwi fruit, using a little grated apple or brown sugar to sweeten the dressing slightly.

Serves 4

59 calories

½ lb (200 g) fresh raw oysters

¼ cup grated daikon radish (2½ oz/70 g) for cleaning oysters

pinch salt

2 tsps rice vinegar

Daikon-Vinegar Dressing

8 trefoil stems for garnish

Cucumber-Daikon Dressing

Grated cucumber and daikon radish are seasoned with lemon juice and salt in this beautiful green dressing. Like Daikon-Vinegar Dressing, this dressing quickly becomes watery and loses its vitamin C. Prepare it as soon as possible before serving.

2 Japanese cucumbers (½ lb/200 g)
1½-inch (4-cm) length daikon radish (3½ oz/100 g)
2–3 Tbsps lemon juice
pinch salt

1. Cut off both ends of the cucumber. Hold the grater, rough side up, over a shallow pan and grate the cucumber with straight, firm strokes.

2. Peel the daikon radish and grate it in the same way over a shallow pan.

3. Transfer the grated cucumber and daikon radish to a colander and allow them to drain naturally for 1–2 minutes.

4. Combine the cucumber and daikon radish in a bowl and mix well.

5. Add the lemon juice and salt and mix thoroughly.

6. Just before serving, add the salad ingredients to the Dressing and mix gently.

Cherry Tomatoes with Cucumber-Daikon Dressing

Wash the cherry tomatoes and remove the stems. Cut each tomato into quarters lengthwise.

Prepare Cucumber-Daikon Dressing as directed above.

Immediately before serving, add the quartered cherry tomatoes to the Dressing, mix gently, and mound in individual dishes.

VARIATIONS AND NOTES

Cucumbers contain digestive enzymes that break down vitamin C, so when using them in a grated dressing, be sure to combine them with vinegar or citrus juices which suppress this process. Cucumber-Daikon Dressing goes well with fish, shellfish, and seaweed. It also complements lighter-flavored mushrooms or even fruit. Try apples, persimmons, or kiwi fruit, using a little grated apple or brown sugar to sweeten the dressing slightly.

Serves 4
23 calories

½ lb (200 g) cherry tomatoes
Cucumber-Daikon Dressing

Pickled Plum Dressing

Umeboshi, pickled plums, are an ancient form of preserved food found even today in most Japanese households. They are often eaten by themselves, but their distinctive, zesty-sour flavor has also made them a popular ingredient in a variety of Japanese dishes. In this dressing, the saltiness of the *umeboshi* is somewhat reduced, and the paste formed by mashing the plums is seasoned with *mirin* and soy sauce. Also know as "Crimson Plum Dressing," it is often used with pale or white vegetables which set off the bright color of the *umeboshi*. This mixture transcends the usual limits for salad dressings and can be used as a delicious sauce for *soba* or *udon* noodles or even spaghetti.

4 pickled plums, with pits
  (1⅓ oz/40 g)
1 Tbsp *mirin*
1 tsp soy sauce

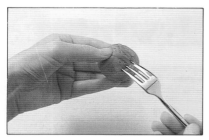

1. Use a fork to make several evenly spaced holes over the surface of each pickled plum.

2. Place the pickled plum in cool water to cover and let soak for two hours, changing the water 2–3 times. This will remove some of the salt.

3. Drain and wipe any excess water from the pickled plums. Pull them apart with your fingers and remove the pits.

4. Force the pickled plums through a fine sieve over a bowl.

5. Add the *mirin* and soy sauce, and mix well.

6. Just before serving, add the salad ingredients to the Dressing and toss.

Celery with Pickled Plum Dressing

Working from the root end, string the celery. Cut each stalk in 1-inch (3-cm) lengths. Thinly slice each of these lengthwise.
  Prepare Pickled Plum Dressing as directed above.
  Before serving, add the celery to the Dressing and toss.

VARIATIONS AND NOTES

The saltiness of pickled plums varies according to the variety. If the recommended soaking time is not long enough to remove the salt from the brand you buy, the saltiness can overpower the pleasant sour flavor of the plums. Adjust the time as needed.
  Almost any light colored vegetable makes a good match with Pickled Plum Dressing both in flavor and presentation: lotus root, mountain yams, potatoes, onions, bean sprouts, cucumber, cauliflower, Chinese cabbage (especially the white part), daikon radish, chicory, and so on. Also good are white fish and tofu.

Serves 4

20 calories

2 stalks celery (½ lb/200 g)
Pickled Plum Dressing

Pickled Plum and Bonito Flake Dressing

This variation of Pickled Plum Dressing adds the flavor of bonito to the salty-sour pickled plum (*umeboshi*). The pickled plum is chopped to bring out the tangy flavor, then seasoned with *mirin* and soy sauce, and thickened with bonito flakes. Since the pickled plum by itself makes a delicious dressing, add as little or much of any of the seasonings as you like.

Some pickled plums contain as much as 20 percent salt. When eaten in large quantities this is an excessive addition of sodium to the diet. Unless you intend to store them for a long time, buy a low-sodium variety.

3 pickled plums, with pits (1 oz/30 g)
1 Tbsp *mirin*
½–1 Tbsp soy sauce
½ cup bonito flakes

1. Pit the pickled plums.

2. Using a large knife, coarsely chop the pitted plums.

3. Transfer the chopped plums to a bowl, add the *mirin* and soy sauce, and fold in. Do not stir the mixture as this will mash the pickled plums.

4. Add the bonito flakes and fold them in. The width of bonito flakes varies. When using a wide variety, parch them and while still hot, wrap them in a dry towel and crumble.

5. Just before serving, combine the salad ingredients and Dressing and toss, being careful not to mash the pickled plums.

Onions with Pickled Plum and Bonito Flake Dressing

Peel and quarter the onion and cut it in very thin slices across the grain. Soak the slices briefly in cool water to remove any bitterness.

Prepare Pickled Plum and Bonito Flake Dressing as directed above.

Just before serving, dry the onions with a towel and combine with the Dressing. Mix gently and arrange in individual dishes.

Serves 4

31 calories

1 onion (½ lb/200 g)
Pickled Plum and Bonito Flake Dressing

VARIATIONS AND NOTES

Like Pickled Plum Dressing, this dressing goes well with light-colored vegetables, green beans, eggplants, and cucumbers. It also complements seafood, *wakame* seaweed, and tofu. Since tofu is easily damaged, the dressing can be served in a separate dish or simply poured on top like a sauce. Try this dressing as a sauce for noodles or even rice.

Sea Urchin Roe Dressing

Sea urchin roe (*uni*) is a highly sought after delicacy in Japan and is priced accordingly. The fresh version is expensive, so processed, bottled sea urchin roe is often used in dressing. The sodium content of packaged brands differs. If you use a low-sodium variety, you may find it necessary to add salt to this recipe. Sea urchin roe makes a very rich dressing and is thus best suited to lighter fish and shellfish. It can also be eaten by itself as an appetizer.

1 Tbsp mashed bottled sea urchin roe

1 egg yolk

1–2 tsps *mirin*

pinch salt

1. Cut a finger-sized cylinder from a daikon radish and round one end. Place the sea urchin roe in a custard cup and, using the cut daikon as a pestle, stir and mash the roe. Continue until liquid from the daikon has thinned the sea urchin roe.

2. Add the egg yolk and continue to dissolve and blend with the daikon radish pestle until the mixture becomes smooth and sticky.

3. Finally, add the *mirin* and mix well. Taste the Dressing and add salt if necessary.

4. Combine the salad ingredients and Dressing immediately before serving.

Note:
If using raw sea urchin roe, place 3½ oz (100 g) of fresh sea urchin in a *suribachi* and grind it with the pestle until smooth. Add 1 tsp light soy sauce and ½ tsp salt and stir to thin the sea urchin roe.

When sea urchin roe loses its freshness, the egg sacs lose their shape and vivid orange color. When buying fresh sea urchin roe, look for uniform grain and color and a firm surface.

Squid with Sea Urchin Roe Dressing

Clean and prepare the squid (see p. 34). Then cut it in thin strips 1½–2 inches (4–5 cm) in length.
   Prepare Sea Urchin Roe Dressing as directed above.
   When ready to serve, combine the Dressing and the squid and mix well. Arrange the squid in individual serving dishes.

VARIATIONS AND NOTES

A variety of seafood is delicious with the subtle flavor of this dressing. Try shrimp, herring roe, whitebait, scallops, and so on. Any light-fleshed fish goes well, as do various vegetables such as daikon radish, mountains yams, and cauliflower. Sea Urchin Roe Dressing can also be used as a sauce for spaghetti or a spread for open-faced sandwiches.

Serves 4

82 calories

1 squid (½ lb/200 g), entrails and tentacles removed

Sea Urchin Roe Dressing

Cod Roe Dressing

Cod roe (*tarako*) is the base for this bright dressing. Seasoned with *mirin* and soy sauce, it makes a flavorful, salty condiment. In general it goes well with light-fleshed fish, shellfish, and the same vegetables recommended for the Sea Urchin Roe Dressing, but here it is combined with green peas for a colorful, eye-pleasing dish. Vegetables dressed with cod roe look best served in small individual dishes.

1 piece lightly salted cod roe
2 tsps *mirin*
1–2 tsps soy sauce

1. Divide the egg sacs (they come in pairs) and cut a lengthwise opening in each sac.

2. Use the edge of the knife to gently scrape out the eggs, being careful not to damage them. Place them in a bowl.

3. Add the *mirin* and the soy sauce.

4. Mix gently until there are no lumps.

5. Just before serving, combine the salad ingredients and the Dressing. Mix gently.

Green Peas with Cod Roe Dressing

Place the peas in ample, salted boiling water and cook until tender. Drain and fan until they have cooled to room temperature.

Prepare Cod Roe Dressing as directed above.

Before serving, combine the peas and the Dressing and mix.

Serves 4

70 calories

½ lb (200 g) shelled green peas
Cod Roe Dressing

VARIATIONS AND NOTES

The roe known as *tarako* in Japan is actually from a fish known as the walleyed pollack (or Alaskan pollack). The roe is sold raw, preserved in salt or even in spicy red pepper (*mentaiko*). In general, *tarako* refers to the salted variety, but there are degrees of saltiness ranging from a lightly salted version meant for immediate consumption to a heavily salted one intended for long-term storage. For this dressing, buy the lightly salted type. Artificial coloring is often added, so choose a roe that is pale pink rather than unnaturally red. Look for intact egg sacs and clearly defined shape.

Fish and shellfish often served with Cod Roe Dressing include squid, abalone, and scallops. When using the dressing with seafood, a dash of citrus juice or vinegar can be added, but this will tend to turn the cod roe somewhat white and cloudy. Suggested vegetables are mountain yams, okra, cucumber, bean sprouts, potatoes, daikon radish, green beans, lotus root, corn, and various types of seaweed. All by itself in a dish, it makes a different and delectable dip.

Vinegar-Soy Dressing

This is the most fundamental dressing of all—a base of vinegar with Japanese seasonings called *ni-haizu*. A sweeter version with *mirin* or brown sugar is *san-baizu*. Dishes dressed with this seasoned vinegar are known as *sunomono* and make up one of the basic categories in Japanese cuisine. Unlike most Western dressings, no oil is used, so the dishes are low in calories. Enjoy to your heart's content.

2 Tbsps rice vinegar
1 Tbsp light soy sauce
pinch salt
3 Tbsps *dashi*

1. In a bowl, combine the rice vinegar, light soy sauce, and salt and beat until the mixture becomes frothy. Add the *dashi* and adjust to taste.

2. Just before serving, add the salad ingredients and mix.

Squash with Vinegar-Soy Dressing

Cut the squash lengthwise in very thin slices and peel the skin from each slice. Cut each slice in 1½–2-inch (4–5-cm) lengths and then julienne each slice with the grain. Sauté the squash briefly in vegetable oil, drain on absorbent paper, and cool to room temperature.

Prepare Vinegar-Soy Dressing as directed above.

Combine the cooled squash with the Dressing just before serving. Toss.

Serves 4
58 calories

10 oz (300 g) winter squash
vegetable oil
Vinegar-Soy Dressing

VARIATIONS AND NOTES

This refreshing dressing complements seafood of all types, vegetables, seaweed, and just about anything else—a true all-purpose dressing. Since the flavor is simple, it can be readily adapted to other seasonings for any number of variations. For example, add ginger (see p. 64) for Ginger Vinegar-Soy Dressing, or *wasabi* horseradish (see p. 64) for *Wasabi* Vinegar-Soy Dressing. Try citrus juice instead of vinegar or create your own version.

Vinegared Egg Yolk Dressing

Vinegar and *mirin* season an egg yolk base which is thickened with the Japanese starch known as *katakuriko*. The result is a Japanese mayonnaise of sorts. Like other rich dressings, it goes well with lighter seafood and vegetables. The bright yellow can be used for appealing color combinations. This dressing is generally served by or over the food rather than mixed with it because when mixed, the visual effect of the vivid yellow is diminished. When arranging the food on dishes, make sure both the dressing and dressed are visible to take full advantage of this contrast.

2 egg yolks
2 Tbsps rice vinegar
4 tsps *mirin*
¼ tsp salt
scant ½ tsp brown sugar
scant ½ tsp *katakuriko* starch
   (or use arrowroot)
2 tsps *dashi* (or water)

2. Set the pan in a larger saucepan half full of boiling water and stir while heating until the mixture thickens to the consistency of mayonnaise. Do not boil. Remove from heat. Arrange salad ingredients in individual serving dishes and pour on the Dressing.

1. In a small bowl, dissolve the *katakuriko* starch in the *dashi*. In a small saucepan, combine the egg yolks, rice vinegar, *mirin*, salt, brown sugar, and *katakuriko-dashi* mixture. Blend well.

Broccoli with Vinegared Egg Yolk Dressing

Break the broccoli into small florets. Drop them in lightly salted boiling water and cook until the broccoli is bright in color and slightly tender. Drain well and let cool.

Prepare the Vinegared Egg Yolk Dressing as directed above.

Arrange the broccoli in individual serving dishes and pour on some of the Dressing.

Serves 4

74 calories

½ lb (200 g) broccoli

pinch salt

Vinegared Egg Yolk Dressing

VARIATIONS AND NOTES

This dressing has the appealing color and texture of mayonnaise without the oil. Use it on shrimp, squid, crab, scallops, and so on. Good vegetable dishes can start with cucumber, alfalfa sprouts, green beans, mountain yams, cauliflower, chicory, asparagus, or artichokes. As with mayonnaise, it does not keep particularly well, but refrigerated will last 2–3 days.

Mustard-Soy Dressing

Mustard is one of the few spices used in traditional Japanese cooking. Here, Japanese mustard (*karashi*) is thinned with *mirin* and flavored with soy sauce for a zesty dressing. Typically it is served with stronger, fishier seafood, but mustard is equally delicious with vegetables. Japanese mustard can be found powdered, in which case, it is reconstituted with an equal amount of lukewarm water before using (see p. 62).

½ tsp reconstituted Japanese mustard (see p. 62)

½ Tbsp *mirin*

1 Tbsp light soy sauce

1. Place the mustard in a bowl and gradually add the *mirin*, stirring gently to dilute. Add the light soy sauce and adjust to taste.

2. Add the salad ingredients to the bowl with the Dressing. Mix gently.

Bean Sprouts with Mustard-Soy Dressing

Add a dash of vinegar to ample boiling water, drop the sprouts in the water, and boil for 2–3 minutes. Drain, immerse in cold water, drain again on a bamboo strainer and sprinkle with the soy sauce. Let cool thoroughly. If you have time and energy to spare, you may want to remove the roots from the sprouts before boiling (see p. 31).

Prepare Mustard-Soy Dressing as directed on the previous page.

Just before serving, thoroughly drain the sprouts. Combine with the Dressing and blend.

VARIATIONS AND NOTES

This dressing is distinctive and flavorful, so combined with other strong flavors it makes for some interesting harmonies. For example, seafood that goes well includes short-necked and hard-shell clams and bonito sashimi. Vegetables often seasoned with mustard are trefoil, lotus root, celery, green beans, alfalfa sprouts, and daikon radish. On the other hand, more lightly flavored foods which tend to take on the mustard flavor are also delicious: squid, crab, white fish, various mushrooms, cabbage, Chinese cabbage, lettuce, and so on.

You can replace the *mirin* with brown sugar if you prefer, or eliminate the sweetness altogether for a simple mustard-soy combination.

Serves 4

17 calories

10 oz (300 g) bean sprouts
dash rice vinegar
1 tsp light soy sauce
Mustard-Soy Dressing

Mustard-Vinegar-Miso Dressing

This dressing starts with sweetish white miso, which is thinned with saké, *mirin*, egg yolk, and rice vinegar. Mustard adds an accent to a popular standard dressing in Japanese cuisine. It is most often served with clams, green onions, and *wakame* seaweed.

For those who prefer a less spicy dressing (and Japanese mustard can be fiery), simply eliminate the mustard. The resulting Vinegar-Miso Dressing is extremely tasty. Enjoy either with a wide variety of seafood and vegetables.

3 Tbsps white miso
1 Tbsp saké
2 tsps *mirin*
1 egg yolk
1 Tbsp rice vinegar
½ tsp reconstituted Japanese mustard (see p. 62)

1. In a saucepan, combine the miso, saké, *mirin*, and egg yolk. Blend until smooth and place over low heat. Using a bamboo rice paddle (or a large wooden spoon), stir the mixture as it heats until it becomes a very thick paste that adheres to the paddle. Remove from heat.

2. Let the miso mixture cool to room temperature, then add the vinegar and mustard. Blend to a smooth consistency. Add additional mustard to suit your taste. Arrange the salad ingredients in individual bowls and pour on the Dressing.

Leeks with Mustard-Vinegar-Miso Dressing

Cut the roots and green ends from the leeks and discard. Slice the white portion in 1½-inch (4-cm) lengths, arrange them in the bottom of a saucepan, and add water to cover. Add the vinegar, cover with a drop-lid (or improvise with a small plate), and simmer over medium heat until the leeks are tender but not too soft.

Prepare the Mustard-Vinegar-Miso Dressing as directed on the previous page.

When ready to serve, drain the leeks, gently pat them dry, and arrange individual portions in serving bowls. Pour some of the Mustard-Vinegar-Miso Dressing over the leeks.

VARIATIONS AND NOTES

This is a sweet dressing, so if you prefer a saltier dressing, experiment with red miso and brown sugar. The sweetness of 1¾ oz/50 g of white miso is equalled by adding 3 Tbsps brown sugar to 1¾ oz/50 g of red miso.

Mustard-Vinegar-Miso Dressing suits seafood—tuna, squid, clams, and so on—and vegetables—trefoil, lettuce, asparagus, broccoli, green beans, eggplant, and so on. It also goes well with *wakame* seaweed.

Serves 4

118 calories

4 large leeks
dash rice vinegar
Mustard-Vinegar-Miso Dressing

Tosa Soy Sauce Dressing

Tosa soy sauce is the common name for the bonito-flavored dressing often used as a dip for sashimi. It is milder than plain soy sauce and has a faint taste of fish. Tosa rice vinegar is similarly bonito flavored.

2 Tbsps soy sauce
2 tsps *mirin*
2 Tbsps bonito flakes

1. Combine the soy sauce, *mirin*, and bonito flakes in a saucepan, bring the mixture to a boil over medium heat, and simmer 4–5 minutes. When the liquid is reduced by approximately 10 percent and the bonito flakes have released some stock, remove the pan from the heat.

2. Place a small strainer over a bowl and strain the mixture to remove the bonito flakes. Let the Dressing cool. When ready to serve, pour the Dressing over the salad ingredients.

Tofu with Tosa Soy Sauce Dressing

Cut the tofu in ⅜-inch (1-cm) cubes.

Prepare the Tosa Soy Sauce Dressing as directed above.

Before serving, drain the tofu well, arrange the cubes in individual dishes, and spoon some Tosa Soy Sauce Dressing over each.

VARIATIONS AND NOTES

Tosa Soy Sauce Dressing can be used instead of *Ohitashi* Dressing (see p. 43), or try a variation of the Vinegar-Soy Dressing (see p. 56) by mixing 4 parts Tosa Soy Sauce Dressing with 6 parts rice vinegar for Tosa Vinegar-Soy Dressing. This is particularly good with white fish, squid, octopus, and shellfish.

Tosa Soy Sauce Dressing can be used with eggplant, zucchini, or onions. It also makes a good, quick marinade for cabbage, carrots, daikon radish, and the like. (Rub these vegetables with salt first to soften them slightly.)

Serves 4

127 calories

2 blocks regular ("cotton") tofu (21 oz/600 g)
Tosa Soy Sauce Dressing

Sesame-Miso Dressing

Sesame seeds ground to a paste are combined with *dashi* and white miso for a richly textured and flavorful dressing. In general, white miso is used with white sesame seeds and red miso with black sesame, but if you prefer a less sweet version of this dressing, use the red.

Sesame-Miso Dressing can also be used as a sauce for boiled daikon radish or grilled eggplant. This miso version is an interesting variation of Sesame Seed Dressing (p. 44).

5½ Tbsps white miso
2 Tbsps *dashi* (or water)
4 Tbsps white sesame seeds

1. Combine the miso and *dashi* in a saucepan, blend to a smooth consistency, and place over low heat. Heat the mixture, stirring constantly, until it stiffens slightly. Let cool.

2. Parch the sesame seeds in a dry frying pan (see p. 44) until they release their aroma, transfer to a dry *suribachi* (or mortar), and grind to a smooth paste. Add the miso-*dashi* mixture and blend well.

Green Beans with Sesame-Miso Dressing

Remove the stems and strings from the beans. Rub them with salt, let stand 1–2 minutes, and drop in ample boiling water. Boil until the color brightens and the beans are just tender (see p. 30). Drain and fan to cool.

Prepare the Sesame-Miso Dressing as directed above.

Cut the green beans in 1-inch (3-cm) lengths, combine with the Dressing, and mix gently.

Serves 4
117 calories

½ lb (200 g) green beans
1 tsp salt
Sesame-Miso Dressing

VARIATIONS AND NOTES

In this variation of Sesame Seed Dressing (p. 44), miso is substituted for the soy sauce. It is simple to prepare and delicious as a dip. Use it with the same ingredients suggested for Sesame Seed Dressing—in particular, leafy greens, daikon radish, and Chinese cabbage.

FLAVORFUL ADDITIONS

Shiso Leaves

Shiso Vinegar-Soy Dressing
Shiso Miso Dressing
Pickled Plum and *Shiso* Dressing
Shiso Vinaigrette
Shiso Mayonnaise

The Japanese are so enamored of the flavor and aroma of *shiso* (perilla leaves) that almost every part of the plant finds its way to the table, not only the leaves, but the flowers, nuts, and so on.

The leaves, particularly abundant in summer, are nutritious—high in vitamins A and C—and also help keep food fresh—a property that makes them the constant companion of raw seafood. When using in dressings, remove the center vein and slice the leaves in narrow strips or chop finely. Add *shiso* to a dressing at the last minute or sprinkle over the top of a dressed salad. Chopped *shiso* in Vinegar-Soy Dressing (p. 56) is *Shiso* Vinegar-Soy Dressing. *Shiso* Miso Dressing is finely chopped *shiso* added to red miso that has been thinned with saké. For Pickled Plum and *Shiso* Dressing, replace the bonito flakes in Pickled Plum and Bonito Flake Dressing (p. 53) with chopped *shiso*. This dressing is just right for tofu, turnips, or daikon radish salads—a flavor combination dear to the heart of nearly every Japanese. As with various other seasonings, *shiso* can be added to vinaigrette or mayonnaise for a novel hybrid creation. Finally, one of the simplest and most appealing uses is simply to chop it finely and mix it with rice or pasta.

Removing the Center Veins: The center veins of *shiso* leaves tend to be tough. Remove them before cutting in strips or chopping. Use a sharp knife to cut the vein away from the leaf halves and pull it out with the stem. If the leaves are particularly young and tender, simply cut off the stems.

Julienning *Shiso*: Remove the center veins from the leaves and roll the halves lengthwise. Slice the rolls in even strips. It is very difficult, if not impossible, to slice the leaf neatly when unrolled.

Wrapping with *Shiso* Leaves: *Shiso* is wonderful chopped or cut and added to dressings, but it has other uses as well. Try wrapping the leaves around vegetables or seafood or tearing them coarsely and including them in a salad. Here julienned daikon radish has been secured with *shiso* leaves. Serve these with Vinegar-Soy Dressing (p. 56) or *Wasabi* Soy Sauce (p. 64).

Japanese Mustard (*Karashi*)

Mustard-Soy Dressing
Mustard-Vinegar-Miso Dressing
Mustard Vinegar-Soy Dressing
Mustard-Miso Dressing
Mustard and Vinegared Egg
Yolk Dressing

Japanese mustard (*karashi*) is generally sold in powdered form. Reconstitute it with an equal amount of lukewarm water. A paste variety is also available in tubes. The Mustard-Soy Dressing (p. 57) and the Mustard-Vinegar-Miso Dressing (p. 58) introduced earlier show how mustard can add spark to dressings. Other ideas include adding Japanese mustard to Vinegar-Soy Dressing (p. 56) for Mustard Vinegar-Soy Dressing or using it to replace the sesame paste in Sesame-Miso Dressing (p. 60) for Mustard-Miso Dressing. Vinegared Egg Yolk Dressing (p. 56) also benefits from the addition of mustard. All these mustard dressings are good with leafy greens, mushrooms, squid, and shrimp and other shellfish.

Reconstituting Mustard: Place the powdered mustard in a deep cup or small bowl and add an equal amount of lukewarm water. Stir and blend quickly. Pay special attention to the temperature of the water. Cold water will not bring out the hotness of the mustard, and hot water stops the action of the enzymes.

Cover the Mustard Briefly: After reconstituting the mustard, cover it and let stand several minutes. It needs a short rest to develop full flavor.

When Adding to Miso: When making either the Mustard-Vinegar-Miso Dressing or the Mustard-Miso Dressing, be sure the miso is room temperature before adding the mustard; the flavor suffers when added to warm ingredients.

Red Chili Peppers (*Togarashi*)

Maple Leaf Grated Daikon Dressing
Nanban Vinegar Dressing
Red Chili Pepper Miso Dressing
Red Chili Pepper Miso and Vinegar-Soy Dressing
Red Chili Pepper Vinaigrette
Red Chili Pepper Mayonnaise

Red chili peppers differ in hotness, but the small variety generally used in Japanese cooking are surely among the most fiery anywhere. The peppers are sold dried and are soaked in lukewarm water to soften before chopping. Always bear in mind that they are extremely hot and you need add only a tiny amount.

The most popular red pepper dressing is Maple Leaf Grated Daikon Dressing. A small hole is hollowed in a daikon radish into which a pepper is inserted. The daikon radish juices soften the pepper and then the two are grated together (see next page). Cutting the pepper in fine rounds and adding it to Vinegar-Soy Dressing (p. 56) yields Nanban Vinegar Dressing, a spicy and delicious dressing. Nanban Vinegar Dressing can also be used as a marinade for fried or grilled fish. In Red Chili Pepper Miso Dressing, the sesame in Sesame-Miso Dressing (p. 60) is replaced by red chili pepper. Use it as a dip or blend it with Vinegar-Soy Dressing (p. 56) for Red Chili Pepper Miso and Vinegar-Soy Dressing.

Red chili peppers are also sold in a powdered form known as *ichimi*. Try adding a small amount of this to vinaigrette or mayonnaise.

Restoring Red Chili Peppers: Remove the stems from the peppers and soak them briefly in lukewarm water to soften. Soaking brings out the full flavor (and flame) and makes for easier chopping.

Removing Seeds: When the pepper has softened, cut a small piece from each end and hold it under water as you knead out the seeds. Slice the skin in thin rounds or chop it finely.

Maple Leaf Grated Daikon: Remove the stem from a red chili pepper. Use a chopstick to poke a hole in the center of a peeled round of daikon radish. Insert the red chili pepper and let stand briefly to allow the pepper to soften and blend with the juice of the daikon. Grate and serve as a condiment with raw or grilled fish or use as a dressing for seafood.

Sansho Sprigs

Sansho Sprig Miso Dressing
Sansho Sprig Vinegar-Soy Dressing
Sansho Sprig Vinaigrette

Sansho sprigs (*kinome*) are young leaves from the *sansho* (prickly ash) tree which arrive at Japanese markets in spring and early summer. Their fresh, young flavor is highly prized as a harbinger of the season of growth. They can be sprinkled over salads or ground in a *suribachi* and combined with miso or vinegar for a luscious dressing. For example, *Sansho* Sprig Miso Dressing can be made by replacing the sesame paste in Sesame-Miso Dressing (p. 60) with *sansho* sprigs that have been partially ground in a *suribachi*. This dressing is good with all sorts of things, including tofu, eggplant, taro, *wakame*, and seafood such as squid, red shell, abalone, shrimp, and octopus. Add ground *sansho* sprigs to Vinegar-Soy Dressing (p. 56) for *Sansho* Sprig Vinegar-Soy Dressing and use it with the ingredients suggested above for fragrant salads. Experiment with *sansho* sprigs. Pluck the leaves, chop them coarsely, and sprinkle over salads as a garnish or add some ground *sansho* sprigs to a vinaigrette and turn it into a pale green sensation.

Releasing Flavor: When using *sansho* sprigs whole, spread one sprig in the palm of your hand and slap it a few times with the other hand. This breaks down cell walls in the buds releasing the wonderful fragrance and flavor. Use *sansho* sprigs prepared in this way as a salad topping.

Grinding *Sansho* Sprigs: Place the *sansho* sprigs, stems and all, in a small *suribachi* and grind until the buds lose their shape. Use a bamboo skewer to scrape the paste from the grooves of the *suribachi*. Mix with miso or rice vinegar to make a dressing.

Scattering *Sansho* Sprigs: One of the most obvious uses for beautiful green *sansho* sprigs is as a spectacular garnish. Pick off the leaves, chop them coarsely, and scatter over salads. The photograph shows a mound of grated mountain yam topped with *sansho* sprigs.

Wasabi Horseradish

Wasabi Soy Sauce
Wasabi Vinegar-Soy Dressing
Wasabi Vinaigrette
Wasabi Mayonnaise

Wasabi horseradish comes from the root of a plant which grows wild in the mountain streams of Japan. The roots are grated to release an elegant, distinctive flavor that is truly Japanese and is a basic element of sushi, sashimi, dips for *soba* noodles, and other traditional dishes. Like ginger, the eye-opening flavor of *wasabi* is a perfect complement for seafood.

Add grated *wasabi* to soy sauce for *Wasabi* Soy Sauce, the best-loved dip for sushi and sashimi. Blending *wasabi* with Tosa Soy Sauce Dressing (p. 59) creates a wonderful seafood dressing. Combine *wasabi* and Vinegar-Soy Dressing (p. 56) to make *Wasabi* Vinegar-Soy Dressing. When the fresh roots are not available, *wasabi* can be purchased as a powder or as a paste.

To reconstitute *wasabi*, place the powdered *wasabi* in a small bowl and add an equal amount of lukewarm water. Stir briskly to create a paste. Cover and allow to set about 10 minutes before using.

Add *wasabi* to a standard vinaigrette or to mayonnaise for East-meets-West dressings.

Wasabi Stems: Before grating the *wasabi* root, scrub it well with a brush and cut off the stems. The stems have already been trimmed from the *wasabi* found in most markets, but if you are lucky enough to find *wasabi* with stems intact, they may be blanched in boiling water, chopped finely and dressed with a little soy sauce for a spicy, delectable, and rare treat.

Peeling Wasabi: The surface of a *wasabi* root is covered with small bumps. Peel the skin thinly as if shaving off these knobs. Peel only the portion of the root you intend to grate and use (*wasabi* is grated from the stem end). Set the *wasabi*, unpeeled, in water to store. Use a fresh root as soon as possible.

Grating Wasabi: Work from the stem end of the root. Use the fine side of the grater and rub the root slowly in a spiraling motion. This grating method releases the maximum flavor and unmistakable *wasabi* aroma. Grated *wasabi* loses its flavor as time passes, so serve it as soon as possible after grating.

Ginger

Ginger Soy Sauce
Ginger Vinegar-Soy Dressing
Ginger-Vinegar-Miso Dressing
Ginger Vinaigrette
Ginger Mayonnaise

Ginger has a slightly hot, heady flavor. It originally came to Japan from more tropical Asian countries. Though ginger is marketed in other forms, in this book ginger means the fresh root.

One of the many properties of this marvelous root is its ability to neutralize less appealing flavors in fish and shellfish. Grated ginger added to soy sauce makes a delicious dip for sashimi. Ginger Vinegar-Soy Dressing is made by adding grated ginger to Vinegar-Soy Dressing (p. 56). For Ginger-Vinegar-Miso Dressing, simply substitute ginger juice for the mustard in Mustard-Vinegar-Miso Dressing (p. 58). Grated ginger or ginger juice can be added to the dressing, or ginger may be cut with the grain in very fine slivers and sprinkled over a salad for added interest. Toss the ginger slivers with the salad before serving.

For an eclectic effect, add grated ginger to a standard vinaigrette, or add grated ginger to mayonnaise for Ginger Mayonnaise.

Peeling Ginger: The skin of a ginger root is thin but rough, following the twisting contour of the root. A knife generally cuts away too much of the skin and with it some of the flavor. Use the edge of a spoon to scrape away the skin and avoid waste.

Grating Ginger: Hold the peeled ginger root firmly and grate it on the coarse side of the grater in straight, firm strokes. Some recipes use both the grated ginger and the juice. Others use only the juice (see right).

Ginger Juice: The texture and appearance of grated ginger root do not suit every recipe—in some cases only the flavor is needed. Place the grated root in a small strainer and use your fingertips to wring out as much of the liquid as possible, catching the fragrant ginger juice in a cup.

Mountain Yams (*Yamaimo*)

Plain Grated Mountain Yam
Sea Urchin with Grated Mountain Yam
Pickled Plum with Grated Mountain Yam

The mountain yam is one of the few varieties of yams that can be eaten raw. It contains an enzyme which helps break down its own starch. In general, the mountain yams that reach the market are either the ginkgo leaf-shaped variety (*icho*) or the long, narrow type (*nagaimo*). Both are delicious but slightly different. The ginkgo leaf-shaped type has a sticky consistency and when grated forms a delightful, oozing, nutritious mass known as *tororo*. The long, narrow type is more watery and chopped makes a good dressing. By themselves, mountain yams have relatively little flavor, but they are good seasoned with *Wasabi* Soy Sauce (facing page) or Tosa Soy Sauce Dressing (p. 59) and served with sashimi, raw oysters, smoked salmon, tofu, or spinach.

Plain Grated Mountain Yam is often used as a dressing on raw fish like tuna. Sea Urchin with Grated Mountain Yam is made by flavoring grated yam with sea urchin paste (see p. 54). Or use pickled plums (see p. 41) and make Pickled Plum with Grated Mountain Yam. These dressings can also be eaten by themselves.

Peeling Mountain Yam: Mountain yams can have a somewhat bitter flavor if not properly prepared. Peel the skins thickly and immediately drop in weak vinegared water to prevent discoloration. When ready to use, drain, rinse, and wipe dry. Yams can be very slippery, so when peeling you may want to leave enough skin on one end to hold while grating.

Grating Mountain Yams: Mountain yams are most easily grated on the grooves of a *suribachi*. Hold the peeled yam firmly and rub it in a circular motion. A grater may be used, but the end product will be roughly textured.

Coarsely Chopping Mountain Yams: First chop the peeled mountain yam coarsely, then using a knife like a cleaver, hack the pieces to bring out their characteristic sticky texture. Add soy sauce, *wasabi* horseradish, or citrus juice to taste for a wonderful dressing.

Tofu and *Natto*

Tofu Dressing
White Vinegar Dressing
Mild Tofu Dressing
Tofu Mayonnaise
Natto Dressing
Natto and Grated Daikon
Natto and Pickled Plums
Natto and Chinese-style Dressing
Natto Mayonnaise

Tofu and *natto* are two of the many wonderful products of the miraculous, nutritious soybean. They assume virtually endless forms in Japanese cooking, including dressings. Tofu Dressing (p. 46) is the most common of these dressings. Another popular choice is White Vinegar Dressing (p. 92), the perfect dressing for daikon radishes, celery, lettuce, and so on, and a great dip for raw vegetables. One dressing idea that actually originated in the United States is to combine tofu, rice vinegar, vegetable oil, and soy sauce in a blender or food processor for Mild Tofu Dressing (see below). Tofu Mayonnaise (p. 109) is a very easy, healthy dressing.

The strong, distinctive flavor of *natto* (fermented soybeans) blends well with soy sauce, miso, pickled plums, and other strong seasonings. Experiment with any of these or your own favorites for original *natto* dressings.

If the *natto* is the large whole-bean variety, chop it coarsely using the knife like a cleaver to bring out the sticky consistency before blending with other ingredients.

Natto Dressing is made by simply adding soy sauce and Japanese mustard to the fermented beans. *Natto* also makes a delicious addition to grated daikon or pickled plums. Chinese-style Dressing (p. 112) or plain mayonnaise both take on new life with a little *natto*.

Mild Tofu Dressing: Combine ½ block (5 oz/150 g) regular ("cotton") tofu, 1 Tbsp rice vinegar, 3–4 Tbsps vegetable oil, scant ½ tsp salt, ½ tsp soy sauce, a little lemon juice, and 3–4 Tbsps heavy cream in a mixer or food processor. Blend at low speed until smooth. Adjust seasonings.

Chopping *Natto*: Before seasoning *natto* for a dressing, it should be chopped coarsely with a large knife or cleaver to bring out the stickiness. For other uses, or for those who object to the sticky consistency *natto* fans prize so much, place the *natto* in a strainer and pour boiling water over it. Drain well and chop as above.

Walnuts

Walnut Dressing
Walnut Vinegar-Soy Dressing
Walnut Vinaigrette
Walnut Mayonnaise

Walnuts, like peanuts, are extremely nutritious. They have as much protein as fish and are rich in fats and vitamin B[1]. Like sesame seeds, they can be ground to a paste and added to dressings. The taste of walnuts goes well with more flavorful vegetables that require strong seasonings. The procedure for Walnut Dressing is the same as that for Sesame Seed Dressing (p. 44). Simply substitute walnut paste for the sesame paste. Walnut Vinegar-Soy Dressing is Vinegar-Soy Dressing (p. 56) seasoned with walnut paste and perhaps some chopped walnuts. Add either chopped walnuts or walnut paste to mayonnaise or vinaigrette for a richer, more flavorful variation.

To remove the thin, paperlike skin from the nuts, soak them briefly in boiling water, drain, and peel.

Walnut Paste

1. Spread the walnuts on a dry, non-terry kitchen towel and chop them coarsely. Remove the thin skin if you prefer.

2. Transfer the walnuts to a dry *suribachi* and grind partially. The walnuts can be used at this stage or ground further.

3. If you continue to grind, the walnuts will release their oil and form a smooth, sticky paste. Add seasonings for a rich, complex dressing.

Nori Seaweed

Nori Dressing
Nori Vinegar-Soy Dressing
Daikon-Vinegar and *Nori* Seaweed
Nori Vinaigrette

Shredded Nori Seaweed (*Kizami-nori*)

Nori, an extremely common seaweed in Japanese food, is made by spreading a type of laver called *amanori* over a rough mat and drying it in sheets.

The dried *nori* sold in stores should be toasted by passing it several times over a low flame until the color brightens before using in sushi or salads. *Nori*, like most seaweeds has virtually no calories, and has abundant vitamins and minerals—what better way to add a naturally healthy and delicious supplement to your daily diet. *Nori* Dressing, *Nori* Vinegar-Soy Dressing, and refreshing Grated Daikon and *Nori* Seaweed are among the dressings that can be created' with *nori*. The simplest and perhaps most appealing use is simply to sprinkle crumbled *nori* over a salad before tossing.

Nori Dressing is made by adding crumbled *nori* to *Wasabi* Soy Sauce (p. 64). Add *nori* to Vinegar-Soy Dressing (p. 56) for *Nori* Vinegar-Soy Dressing; to Daikon-Vinegar Dressing (p. 50) for Daikon-Vinegar and *Nori* Seaweed. And, of course, *nori* seaweed in a vinaigrette gives a new meaning to East-meets-West. Serve *nori* dressings with any vegetable and most seafood (squid, shrimp, or oysters are particularly tasty).

Toasting *Nori*: Hold two sheets of *nori* together, right sides in, and toast by quickly passing several times over a low flame until the *nori* turns a brighter green. The right side of *nori* seaweed is shiny, and the wrong side is rough and bears the imprint of the drying rack.

Crumbled *Nori* Seaweed: When toasted, *nori* seaweed becomes dry and crumbly. Place it in a dry towel or a plastic bag and crush it in fine pieces. Crumbled *nori* is a boon to salads or soups.

***Nori* Seaweed Strips:** After toasting the *nori*, while still hot, crease the sheet in 1½–2-inch (4–5-cm) wide strips and tear it apart (some *nori* comes perforated). Stack the strips and use dry kitchen scissors to cut off slivers from the end of the stack. *Nori* seaweed strips are beautiful and delectable sprinkled over cold *soba* or *udon* noodles.

Green Onions and Long Onions

Green/Long Onion Vinegar-Miso Dressing
Green/Long Onion Vinegar-Soy Dressing
Green/Long Onion Vinaigrette
Green/Long Onion Mayonnaise

Green onions and the long onions common in Japan, like the familiar yellow onion, belong to the lily family. Their special aroma stimulates the appetite and helps disguise the strong flavor of raw fish. While both types of onion taste alike and may be used interchangeably, different parts of each onion are consumed. Usually the tender white part of the long onion is eaten and the leaves are discarded, but the green onion is appreciated mainly for its green leaves.

Cut long onions in fine strips or chop green onions coarsely and sprinkle on top of a salad. Or finely chop either type of onion and mix with miso and/or vinegar to make a dressing. Particularly successful combinations are Green/Long Onion Vinegar-Miso Dressing and Green/Long Onion Vinegar-Soy Dressing, which both go well with light seafood and vegetables. Green/Long Onion Vinegar-Miso Dressing is made by substituting chopped green or long onions for the mustard in Mustard-Vinegar-Miso Dressing (p. 58). When using green onions you may want to grind them in a *suribachi* before adding them. Green/Long Onion Vinegar-Soy Dressing is Vinegar-Soy Dressing (p. 56) with chopped green or long onions added. Like yellow onions, green or long onions may also be chopped and added to vinaigrette or mayonnaise.

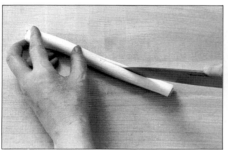

Finely Chopping the Long Onion: Cut off as much as you plan to use. Make several long lengthwise cuts in the white base of the onion. For easier chopping, do not cut all the way through the roots. Chop, starting at the cut end. To chop more finely, hold down the tip of the knife with your left hand and move the blade up and down with your right.

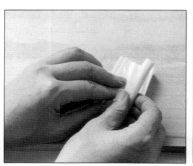

Julienning the Long Onion: Cut the white base of the onion in 1½–2-inch (4–5 cm) lengths. Cut the pieces in half lengthwise and remove the yellowish center. Slice the pieces lengthwise in narrow strips and drop them in cool water. This removes some of the bitterness and brings out the luster of the long onion. Drain well before using.

BEAUTIFUL SALADS

A First Course Salad

Shrimp and *Wakame* Seaweed with Vinegared Egg Yolk Dressing

Photograph on page 9

This dressing owes its appeal to the bright yellow of the egg yolks. While it has about the same consistency as mayonnaise, it has none of the oil. The taste is mild, light, and pleasing, and the festive color combination makes this dish ideal for entertaining.

1. Devein the shrimp (see p. 35). Bring 4 cups of water to a boil in a saucepan, add the rice vinegar, then add the shrimp and return to a boil. Simmer just until the shrimp turn bright pink, remove from heat, and let set 1 minute. Drain. When the shrimp have cooled enough to be handled comfortably, remove the shells leaving the heads and tails intact.

2. Place the *wakame* seaweed in a strainer and pour boiling water over it. Immerse in cold water. Drain and squeeze out the excess liquid. Cut away the tough vein in the *wakame* and cut it in bite-sized pieces.

3. Wash the daikon sprouts thoroughly and cut off the roots.

4. Combine the egg yolks and *katakuriko* starch in a small saucepan (or the top of a double boiler), add the *dashi*, and mix gently. Add the rice vinegar, *mirin*, salt, and brown sugar. Boil water in a somewhat larger saucepan (or the bottom of the double boiler) and place the smaller pan in the larger. Heat gradually, stirring constantly, until the mixture thickens to the consistency of mayonnaise.

5. Blend the ingredients for the Coating Vinegar. Add the shrimp, coat well, and remove immediately. Do the same with the *wakame* seaweed.

6. Pour ¼ of the Vinegared Egg Yolk Dressing on each dish, add 2 shrimp and some *wakame*. Top with daikon sprouts before serving.

Serves 4
88 calories

8 large shrimp
1 Tbsp rice vinegar
1¾ oz (50 g) restored *wakame* seaweed (see p. 32)
40 stalks daikon sprouts (*kaiware daikon*) (1¾ oz/50 g)

Vinegared Egg Yolk Dressing

2 egg yolks
scant ½ tsp *katakuriko* starch (or use arrowroot)
2–3 tsps *dashi* (or water)
1–2 Tbsps rice vinegar
4 tsps *mirin*
¼ tsp salt
scant ½ tsp brown sugar

Coating Vinegar

2 Tbsps rice vinegar
2 Tbsps *dashi*
dash light soy sauce
scant ½ tsp salt

Salads for a Buffet

Cauliflower with Sea Urchin Mayonnaise

Photograph on page 10

The pale, appetizing color of this dressing comes from blending bright orange sea urchin roe with yellow egg yolk in a mayonnaise

Serves 4
161 calories

69

base. This is not a heavily spiced dressing, but its richness combines with the texture of the cauliflower for a memorable salad.

1. Separate the cauliflower into small florets. Add the salt and rice vinegar to ample boiling water. Add the cauliflower and cook until just tender, drain, and let cool.

2. Place the sea urchin roe in a bowl, add the egg yolk, and blend thoroughly. Add the mayonnaise and stir well to form a smooth paste.

3. Combine the cauliflower and the Mayonnaise and mix gently. Transfer to a serving dish and sprinkle with the chopped parsley.

½ head cauliflower (10 oz/300 g)

pinch salt

dash rice vinegar

Sea Urchin Mayonnaise

1½ Tbsps salted bottled sea urchin roe (see p. 54)

1 egg yolk

5 Tbsps mayonnaise

1 tsp chopped parsley

Turnips and Apricots in Sweet Vinegar Dressing

Photograph on page 10

The unassuming, subtle flavor of turnips goes surprisingly well with the strong sweet-and-sour taste of dried apricots. This salad is conceptually and nutritionally appealing as well—a fresh, white root vegetable matured in the darkness of the earth paired with a tree-ripened, sun-dried fruit.

1. Cut the turnips in very thin quarter-rounds (see p. 28).

2. Cut the apricots crosswise into ⅛-inch (5-mm) slices. (If they are too hard, sprinkle some Dressing on them to soften before combining with the other ingredients.)

3. Drop the turnip stems in boiling water and cook until the color brightens and they are tender. Remove, soak briefly in cold water, then drain. Squeeze out the excess water. Cut in 1½-inch (4-cm) lengths.

4. Combine the Dressing ingredients and blend thoroughly. Add the turnip, apricot, and turnip stems, toss well, and transfer to serving dishes.

Serves 4

91 calories

3 turnips, without tops (10 oz/300 g)

2½ oz (70 g) dried apricots

1 oz (30 g) turnip stems

Sweet Vinegar Dressing

3 Tbsps rice vinegar

3 Tbsps *mirin*

¼ tsp salt

Broccoli with *Konbu* Tea Dressing

Photograph on page 10

Boiled broccoli is dressed with *konbu* tea for a very easy salad. *Konbu* tea is made by drying *konbu* kelp and then reducing it to powder for a naturally salty tea. There are no other spices, just the broccoli with the salt and scent of the ocean.

1. Cut the broccoli into florets, discarding any tough stems. Bring an ample amount of lightly salted water to a boil, add the broccoli, and cook until just barely tender. Drain well.

2. While the broccoli is still hot, sprinkle with the *konbu* tea.

Serves 4

26 calories

10 oz (300 g) broccoli

pinch salt

2 tsps *konbu* tea

Konbu Tea: To make *konbu* tea (sold as "kombu powder"), *konbu* kelp is sun-dried and ground. It has a naturally salty taste. Add hot water to make tea or mix it with parched sesame seeds and sprinkle it on hot rice. Or use it as a salad seasoning.

Daikon Radish and Kiwi Fruit Salad

Photograph on page 11

The sharp tang of daikon radish and the sweetness of kiwi, with just a hint of soy sauce, make for another delicious, refreshing salad.

1. Cut the daikon radish in very thin quarter-rounds (see p. 28). Immerse them briefly in cold water to bring out their crispness.
2. Peel the kiwi fruits, and slice in ¼-inch (5-mm) quarter-rounds.
3. Drain the daikon, wrap in a kitchen towel, pat dry, and place in a colander. Sprinkle with a small amount of vegetable oil and drain thoroughly.
4. Combine the Vinaigrette ingredients and mix thoroughly. Add the daikon radish and kiwi fruit. Mix. Arrange in a serving dish. Top with the almond slivers.

Serves 4

158 calories

3-inch (8-cm) length daikon radish (½ lb/200 g)

2 kiwi fruits

vegetable oil

Soy Vinaigrette

2 Tbsps rice vinegar

4 Tbsps vegetable oil

pinch salt

2 tsps light soy sauce

1 Tbsp toasted almond slivers

Tomato Appetizer

Photograph on page 11

With a simple mixture of vegetables, strong or heavy seasonings are often less appropriate than the mild flavor of just a touch of rice vinegar and soy sauce. The lighter dressing shows the freshness and natural goodness of the vegetables to their best advantage. The dressing for this salad is a case in point—it uses no oil and no salt. The bonito flakes and strong flavor of the raw onion were seemingly made for each other.

1. Remove the stems from the tomatoes and cut each tomato crosswise in 4 slices of equal thickness.
2. Slice the onion thinly crosswise and soak briefly in cool water. Drain.
3. Dry the onion and arrange onion slices and then daikon sprouts on top of each tomato slice. Sprinkle with bonito flakes.
4. Combine Dressing ingredients and mix well. Before serving, pour the Dressing over each appetizer.

Serves 4

27 calories

2 tomatoes

½ onion (choose one slightly smaller than the tomatoes)

¼ cup daikon sprouts (*kaiware daikon*), cut in ½-inch (1.5-cm) lengths

2 Tbsps bonito flakes

Vinegar-Soy Sauce Dressing

1 Tbsp rice vinegar

1 Tbsp soy sauce

Salads as Appetizers

Okra with Flavorful Cod Roe Dressing

Photograph on page 12

The cod roe (*tarako*) used in this dressing is lightly salted, so additional flavorings are kept to a minimum—saké and soy sauce. This variation of the dressing on page 55 uses saké instead of *mirin* to better complement the okra. Choose tiny, young okra.

1. Rub the okra with salt to remove the tiny hairs and cook in boiling water until the pods turn a brighter green and are tender. Drain, place in a colander and fan until cool. This preserves the green color. Cut the okra in ¾-inch (2-cm) lengths.
2. Make a vertical incision in each egg sac of the cod roe and use the edge of the knife to carefully scrape out the eggs. Transfer the eggs to a small bowl, add the saké, and mix gently. Add soy sauce to taste. As the cod itself is quite salty, not much soy sauce will be necessary.
3. Combine the okra and the Dressing and serve.

Serves 4

28 calories

½ lb (200 g) okra

salt

Flavorful Cod Roe Dressing

1 piece lightly salted cod roe

1–2 Tbsps saké

dash soy sauce

Mountain Yam with Green Seaweed Flakes

Photograph on page 12

The mountain yam (*nagaimo*) is a unique and appealing tuber with a crispy white flesh that produces a viscous substance when cut. Unlike many tubers, mountain yams are actually better for the digestion eaten raw as they are high in diastase. Green seaweed flakes (*ao-nori*) are made from dried and processed seaweed.

1. Wash the mountain yam, cut it in 2-inch (5-cm) lengths and remove the skin. Soak for about 20 minutes in vinegared water (1 Tbsp rice vinegar to every cup water) to cover, drain, and pat dry. Chop coarsely and mound on four dishes.

2. Make an indentation in the center of the mound and carefully break a quail egg into the hollowed out area. This can be done most easily by cutting away the round, thick end of the egg with a sharp knife and pouring out the contents over the mountain yam. Finally, sprinkle the green seaweed flakes in a line over the quail egg and mountain yam.

3. Before eating, add soy sauce to taste and thoroughly mix the mountain yam, quail egg, and green seaweed flakes.

Serves 4

75 calories

10 oz (300 g) mountain yam

2 cups vinegared water for mountain yam

4 quail eggs

green seaweed flakes

dash soy sauce

Green Seaweed Flakes (Ao-nori): Green seaweed flakes (sold as "green nori flakes") are a popular condiment or garnish for salads and soups. *Ao-nori* is harvested from the same shallow coastal waters as *nori* seaweed, then sun-dried and crushed into flakes.

Red Shell with Mustard-Vinegar-Miso Dressing

Photograph on page 12

Red shell (*akagai*) has a beautiful crimson color and an elegant, subtle flavor that make it a perfect choice for sushi or sashimi. In Japan, seafood is usually served with daikon radish or cucumber cut into fine strings. Recently it has been found that nutrition-wise, these raw vegetables complement the seafood.

1. Remove the meat from the shell (see p. 33). Transfer the meat to a colander, sprinkle with salt, and shake vigorously to remove the viscous, sticky coating. Transfer to a bowl and wash thoroughly. Let stand in cold water for about 2 minutes to remove odor and soften the meat.

2. Pat the red shell dry and cut into bite-sized pieces. Sprinkle with 1 tsp of the vinegar.

3. Cut the cucumbers into pieces about 2 inches (5 cm) long and julienne. Soak in cold water to crisp.

4. Wash the salt from the *tosakanori* seaweed and soak it in very lightly salted water. When the saltiness is somewhat reduced, drain and wrap the seaweed in a towel and shake off the excess water.

5. In a small saucepan, combine all the Dressing ingredients except for the mustard and place over low heat. Warm the mixture slowly, stirring constantly and being careful not to let it boil. When the Dressing approaches a boil, immediately remove from heat. Cool to room temperature. Add the mustard and blend well.

6. Drain the cucumber, add 1 tsp rice vinegar, and stir to coat completely.

7. Arrange portions of the red shell, cucumber, and *tosakanori* on individual dishes and top with the Dressing just before serving.

Serves 4

90 calories

4 red shells

1 Tbsp salt

2 tsps rice vinegar

1½ Japanese cucumbers (5 oz/150 g)

1¾ oz (50 g) fresh *tosakanori* seaweed (or use dulse)

Mustard-Vinegar-Miso Dressing

5½ Tbsps white miso

2 tsps saké

2 tsps *mirin*

2 tsps–1 Tbsp rice vinegar

1 Tbsp *dashi* (or water)

½–1 tsp reconstitued Japanese mustard (see p. 62)

Orange Baskets

Photograph on page 13

This wonderful appetizer is a symphony of colors, aromas, and textures. The faint suggestion of soy sauce gives the seaweed just the right flavor, the trefoil provides a colorful and fragrant accent, and the scent of oranges encompasses all.

1. Slice two wedge-shaped pieces from the upper half of each orange, leaving a strip resembling a basket handle (see photograph on p. 13). Remove the flesh, being careful not to damage the basket handle. Remove the membranes on the segments and break the flesh up into small pieces with your hands.

2. Cut the roots off the trefoil. Drop in boiling water briefly, remove, and immerse in cold water. Drain and cut in ¾-inch (2-cm) pieces.

3. Place the *wakame* seaweed in a colander and douse it with boiling water. Immerse in cold water and drain well. Cut off the vein if tough and chop in 1-inch (3-cm) pieces.

4. Combine the Dressing ingredients and blend.

5. Divide the orange flesh in half (reserve half for another use). Combine half the orange flesh, the trefoil, and the *wakame* seaweed with the Dressing and blend well.

6. Fill the orange baskets with the mixture and serve.

Serves 4

61 calories

4 medium oranges

2–3 stalks trefoil

⅓ oz (10 g) restored *wakame* seaweed (see p. 32)

Dressing

2 Tbsps rice vinegar

2 tsps light soy sauce

2 Tbsps orange juice

pinch salt

Avocado and Shrimp Salad

Photograph on page 13

This salad is beautiful and at the same time practical. Avocado is combined with shrimp, then returned to the avocado skin for serving. Lemon juice prevents this discoloration.

1. Devein the shrimp (see p. 35). Bring ample water to boil in a saucepan and add the salt and the rice vinegar. Boil the shrimp very briefly—30 seconds should be enough—just until they turn bright pink. Drain immediately and let them cool. Remove the heads and shells and squeeze a little lemon juice over the shrimp.

2. Slice the avocados in half lengthwise. Remove the pits. Use a large spoon to scrape the flesh from the peel in large pieces. Reserve the peel. Cut the avocado flesh in ½-inch (1.5-cm) cubes and sprinkle with lemon juice.

3. Combine all the Vinaigrette ingredients, mix well, and add the shrimp and cubed avocado. Blend gently but thoroughly.

4. Return the mixture to the avocado peels and top with a small amount of cottage cheese.

Serves 4

256 calories

8 shrimp

pinch salt

dash rice vinegar

lemon juice for shrimp

2 medium avocados

lemon juice for avocados

Soy Vinaigrette

2 Tbsps rice vinegar

4 Tbsps vegetable oil

pinch salt

2 tsps light soy sauce

1 Tbsp cottage cheese

Smoked Salmon with Rape Flower Dressing

Photograph on page 13

Smoked salmon has a wonderful flavor all its own that doesn't need help from a strong dressing. Rape Flower Dressing is simply egg yolks cooked to a crumbly consistency. The bright yellow recalls the rape flowers that decorate spring fields in Japan.

1. Place the egg yolk in a small saucepan or the top of a double boiler and beat lightly. Add salt and place the small pan in a slightly larger one half full of boiling water (or over the bottom of the double boiler). Cook the egg, stirring constantly, until it reaches a fine, crumbly consistency. Pinch a small amount of the egg—it should be

Serves 4

97 calories

Rape Flower Dressing

1 egg yolk

pinch salt

8 thin slices smoked salmon

4 chrysanthemum leaves (optional)

8 capers

somewhat elastic. Remove from heat. Force the egg through a fine sieve. As an alternative to this double boiler method, a similar effect can be achieved by forcing the yolk of a hard-boiled egg through a fine sieve. (Do not add salt.)

2. Rub the egg yolk over both sides of each slice of salmon and roll each slice up.

3. Arrange the rolls on a serving plate and garnish with chrysanthemum leaves. Top each roll with a caper.

Main Dish Salads

Rice Salad

Photograph on page 14

Even today it is no exaggeration to say that rice plays the central role in virtually every Japanese meal. This Rice Salad is a version of scattered sushi (*chirashi-zushi*). This festive mixture of vinegared rice, seafood, and vegetables is a good choice for home entertaining.

1. Wash the rice until the water runs clear, then soak it in cold water for 30 minutes. Drain well and transfer to a heavy-bottomed saucepan. Add 1⅔ cups (400 ml) of cold water and the saké, and cook (see pp. 36–37).

2. After the rice has finished cooking, let it stand, covered, for 8 minutes, then transfer it to a large wooden bowl or sushi tub. Combine the Dressing ingredients, blend well, and gradually pour over the hot rice. As you pour, mix in the Dressing with a wooden spoon or rice paddle using a chopping motion. Fan the rice to cool it to room temperature.

3. Remove any shell or cartilage from the crabmeat.

4. String the celery and cut it in ¼-inch (5-mm) cubes.

5. Wipe the caps of the shiitake mushrooms with a slightly damp paper towel and cut off the ends of the stems. Sprinkle a little salt on the white undersides of the caps and grill the mushrooms briefly. Slice them in ¼-inch (5-mm) wide strips.

6. Beat the eggs lightly in a saucepan, add the salt and saké, and place over medium heat. Cook the eggs, stirring constantly and rapidly with a fork or several chopsticks held in one hand until they have set. Do not overcook.

7. Combine the rice, crab, celery, shiitake mushrooms, and egg, and mix well. Transfer to a serving dish.

Serves 6

260 calories

2 cups short-grain white rice (11 oz/320 g)

1 Tbsp saké

Sushi Salad Dressing

3 Tbsps rice vinegar

1 Tbsp vegetable oil

1 tsp salt

1 Tbsp brown sugar

4 oz (120 g) canned crabmeat

1 stalk celery

10 fresh shiitake mushrooms (3½ oz/100 g)

pinch salt

2 eggs

another pinch salt

1 tsp saké

Clams with Ginger-Soy Dressing

Photograph on page 14

Compared to meat or even fish, shellfish has very little fat. Here is a simple, savory way to enjoy clams. Buy the freshest ones possible, steam them very briefly, and add a fragrant gingery soy sauce dressing.

1. Soak the clams in moderately salty water overnight. This will cause them to expel any sand (see p. 33).

2. Wash the shells thoroughly, transfer them to a deep saucepan, and sprinkle with saké. Cover and place over medium heat. Steam until the shells open. Discard any clams that do not open.

Serves 4

35 calories

1 lb (500 g) fresh clams in the shell

salt

2 Tbsps saké

Ginger-Soy Dressing

1 tsp ginger juice (see p. 64)

2 tsps soy sauce

3. Combine the Dressing ingredients. About 30 seconds after the shells open in the deep saucepan, add the Dressing and stir well. Remove from heat.

4. Slice the lemon in very thin quarter-rounds (see p. 28).

5. Transfer the clams to a serving dish. You may find that removing the meat from about half the clams and discarding their shells makes for easier presentation. Garnish with lemon and chopped *shiso* leaves.

½ lemon

½ tsp finely chopped *shiso* leaves

White Fish Salad

Photograph on page 15

This salad combines white fish, vegetables, potato chips, and some nuts in a very substantial salad. The dressing contains sesame oil, ginger, and soy sauce—rich and slightly Chinese in mood. Serve the salad as a snack with cocktails or add rice or bread for a light meal. If you prefer, substitute other sashimi-quality raw seafood such as sweet shrimp (*amaebi*) or squid for the white fish.

1. Slice the fish in very thin, diagonal slices (see p. 35).

2. String the celery and cut it in 1-inch (3-cm) lengths. Thinly slice each piece.

3. Coarsely chop the cashews.

4. Tear the lettuce into bite-sized pieces.

5. Crumble the potato chips into pieces roughly the size of the chopped cashews.

6. Coarsely chop the parsley.

7. Julienne the green onions.

8. Combine the Dressing ingredients and mix well.

9. Combine all the fish, celery, cashews, lettuce, potato chips, parsley, and green onions, toss well, and add the Dressing just before serving.

Serves 4

237 calories

½ lb (200 g) white fish fillet (sashimi-quality sea bream, flounder, halibut, sole, etc.)

½ stalk celery

¼ cup cashews

½ small head lettuce

1 cup crumbled potato chips

2–3 sprigs parsley

2 green onions

Chinese Mood Dressing

1 Tbsp rice vinegar

3 Tbsps light soy sauce

¾ tsp ginger juice (see p. 65)

2 Tbsps sesame oil

½ tsp parched white sesame seeds

Portable Salads

Cabbage and Carrot Layers

Photograph on page 16

This one looks like a lot of work but once the chopping is done it's really quite simple. The vegetables are sprinkled with salt and pressed in layers. The salt brings out the flavor of each vegetable, and the layering mingles them into a subtle, delectable, and eye-pleasing dish.

1. Wash the cabbage and carrots and julienne both. Place them in separate bowls, and add 1 tsp salt to the cabbage and ½ tsp salt to the carrots.

2. Spread plastic wrap in a shallow pan or on any flat surface and arrange a bottom layer of 4 *shiso* leaves. On this, spread a layer of cabbage, then carrots, and another layer of *shiso*. Repeat, in that order, for four layers, ending with *shiso* leaves. Cover with plastic wrap, and weight with a heavy object (4 or 5 plates will work). Let stand overnight.

3. Just before serving, unwrap and cut in 1-inch (3-cm) squares.

Serves 4

40 calories

¼ head cabbage (1 lb/450 g)

1½ carrots (5 oz/150 g)

1½ tsps salt

20 *shiso* leaves

Salted Turnips with Raisins and Lemon

Photograph on page 16

This is a slightly salty, refreshing marinated salad with a hint of soy sauce, lemon, and—for a novel touch—some rum. But the lightness of the dressing lets the flavors of the vegetables shine through.

1. Cut the stems from the turnips leaving about ¾-inch (2-cm). Cut the turnips in half lengthwise and slice them, also lengthwise, in very thin slices. Sprinkle with the salt and let stand 5–10 minutes. When the turnip slices have become slightly soft and flexible, gently squeeze out any excess moisture with your hands. Sprinkle with light soy sauce.

2. Slice the lemon in very thin quarter-rounds (see p. 28).

3. Rinse the raisins in water, drain, and place them in a saucepan. Sprinkle with the rum and place over medium heat until the rum evaporates. Remove from heat and let cool to room temperature.

4. Combine the turnips, lemon, and raisins and mix well. Arrange in a serving dish.

Serves 4
29 calories

2 turnips (½ lb/200 g)
½ tsp salt
1 tsp light soy sauce
½ lemon
2 Tbsps raisins
dash rum

Sardines in Nanban Vinegar-Ginger Dressing

Photograph on page 16

Adding red chili pepper and a little sweetness to the standard Vinegar-Soy Dressing (page 56) yields Nanban Vinegar-Ginger Dressing. Here saké has been used instead of *dashi*, and ginger has been added. This dressing is often used as a marinade for deep-fried sardines, mackerel, squid, and so on, because the soy sauce and ginger add a refreshing and aromatic touch that is perfect for fish.

1. Use your thumbs to rub the scales off each sardine. Cut away each head and make a small cut in the belly and remove the entrails. Wash thoroughly and cut in 1½-inch (4-cm) lengths.

2. Lay the sardines in a colander, sprinkle with salt, and let drain for 30 minutes.

3. Combine the Dressing ingredients in a saucepan, blend thoroughly, and place over medium heat. Bring to a boil and remove from heat.

4. Cut both ends from the red chili pepper. Remove the seeds and discard. Chop in several pieces.

5. Peel the ginger root and cut in thin slices.

6. Pat the sardines dry with paper towels and dredge them lightly in flour. Shake off any excess flour.

7. Heat the vegetable oil to 340°F (170°C).

8. Drop the sardines in the hot oil and deep-fry until golden brown. Drain on absorbent paper and transfer to a serving dish.

9. Add the chopped pepper and ginger to the Dressing and return to a boil. Pour the hot Dressing over the sardines. Let soak for about 30 minutes. If you prefer a spicier version, marinate for up to a full day.

10. Julienne the celery and carrot. To serve, place some celery and carrot on each plate, arrange sardines on top, and spoon on some Dressing.

Serves 4
243 calories

1 lb (500 g) sashimi-quality sardines
salt

Nanban Vinegar-Ginger Dressing
5 Tbsps rice vinegar
3 Tbsps brown sugar
5 Tbsps light soy sauce
3 Tbsps saké

1 red chili pepper
½ oz (15 g) ginger root
flour
vegetable oil for deep-frying
½ stalk celery
1-inch(3-cm)piece carrot(⅔ oz/20g)

HEALTHY SALADS

Light Salads

Lotus Root with Pickled Plum Dressing

Photograph on page 17

Lotus root is a high-fiber root vegetable that has long been used in China and Japan as a preventative for gastro-intestinal, throat, and tracheal diseases. Dress it up with pickled plum, also long held to be medicinal, and you have what might be called the quintessential health salad.

1. Wash the lotus root thoroughly and cut it in 1½–2-inch (4–5-cm) lengths. Peel the skin, sometimes cutting lengthwise grooves between the rounded curves of the openings so that when sliced in rounds the edges will be scalloped like the petals of a flower. Slice in ¼-inch (5-mm) rounds. Drop the lotus in vinegared water (1 Tbsp rice vinegar for every cup water) to cover and soak.

2. Bring ample water to boil in a saucepan and add a dash of rice vinegar. Add the lotus root and boil until its color changes. Drain and pat dry.

3. Remove the pits from the pickled plums and force the flesh through a fine sieve. Transfer to a small bowl, add the *mirin* and soy sauce and mix well.

4. Combine the lotus root and Dressing, mix thoroughly, and arrange in a serving dish.

Serves 4

23 calories

6-inch (15-cm) length lotus root (3½ oz/100 g) (look for one that is not too thick)

vinegared water for lotus root

dash rice vinegar

Pickled Plum Dressing

2 pickled plums, with pits (⅔ oz/20g) (soaked in water 1–2 hours)

1½ tsps *mirin*

½ tsp soy sauce

Tomato and Watercress Salad with Japanese-style Dressing

Photograph on page 17

Watercress has approximately three times as much calcium as spinach. It is good raw or sautéed. This salad adds tomatoes and mushrooms and a soy-flavored dressing.

1. Wash the watercress and cut away the tough lower stems.

2. Cut the stems from the tomatoes. Cut the tomato as if cutting it in eighths, being careful not to slice all the way through to the bottom, and open it out like a flower.

3. Slice the mushrooms vertically into thin slices and sprinkle with lemon juice.

4. Combine the Dressing ingredients and mix well.

5. Divide the watercress among the serving dishes, reserving about 4 sprigs. Spread it in a thin layer and place a tomato in the center. Fill the tomato with mushroom slices, and add a sprig of watercress. Spoon the Dressing over the salad just before eating.

Serves 4

155 calories

1 bunch watercress (3½ oz/100 g)

4 tomatoes

8 button mushrooms

2 tsps lemon juice

Japanese-style Dressing

2 Tbsps rice vinegar

4 Tbsps vegetable oil

1 Tbsp soy sauce

1 Tbsp chopped green onions

pinch brown sugar

77

Green Pepper with Chopped Sesame Dressing

Photograph on page 17

Peppers are different from most vegetables. Instead of peeling the skin to eat what is inside, you simply discard the seeds inside and eat the nourishing outside "skin." However, sesame is just the opposite—you eat the tiny seeds which contain a condensed dose of calcium, protein, and nutritious fats. These opposites attract for a delicious salad which needs only the lightest touch of soy sauce to bring out the natural goodness of the ingredients.

1. Grill the peppers whole just until they begin to scorch. Turn frequently to cook evenly. Remove from heat and slice each pepper in 4–6 wedges, remove the stem and seeds and discard. While the pepper is still hot, sprinkle with the soy sauce.
2. Coarsely chop the sesame seeds (see p. 45).
3. Combine the green pepper and chopped sesame and blend well. Transfer to a serving dish.

Serves 4

37 calories

2 green peppers (½ lb/200 g)
2 tsps soy sauce

Chopped Sesame Dressing

2 Tbsps black sesame seeds

Root Vegetable Salads

Burdock and Sesame Salad

Photograph on page 18

Burdock root is full of fiber, and it also prevents constipation. Beating the root softens the fiber, making it easier for the flavors of sesame, rice vinegar, and soy sauce to be absorbed.

1. To make the Dressing, parch the sesame seeds (see p. 44), transfer to a *suribachi* or mortar, and grind to a coarse paste. Add the rice vinegar, brown sugar, and soy sauce and blend well.
2. Use a scrub brush to wash the burdock thoroughly. Cut it in approximately 8-inch (20-cm) lengths. Cut the thicker roots in half lengthwise. Place in vinegared water (1 tsp rice vinegar for every cup water).
3. Combine the Simmering Liquid ingredients in a large saucepan and place over medium-high heat. Drain the burdock root and add to the pan. Simmer 3–4 minutes. The root should still be quite firm.
4. Drain the burdock and place it on a cutting board. Use the pestle from the *suribachi*, a wooden mallet, or any other heavy object to beat the burdock root until it is soft and pliable. Cut in 1½-inch (4-cm) lengths.
5. While the burdock is still warm, add it to the *suribachi* with the Dressing and combine thoroughly. Let cool to room temperature.

Serves 4

55 calories

Sesame Dressing

2 Tbsps black (or white) sesame seeds
2 tsps rice vinegar
½ Tbsp brown sugar
2 tsps soy sauce

4 oz (120 g) fresh burdock root (use thin ones)

vinegared water for burdock

Simmering Liquid

4 Tbsps *dashi*
1 tsp brown sugar
1 tsp rice vinegar
2 tsps soy sauce

Daikon Radish and Carrots with *Shiso* Dressing

Photograph on page 18

This excellent salad is beautiful, simple, and redolent with the fresh fragrance of *shiso*. Both daikon radish and carrots are so nutritious and delicious that the government should set minimum daily requirements. It is well known that cooking carrots in a little oil improves absorption of vitamin A, but they are almost equally as good eaten raw—they are even said to reduce fatigue.

Serves 4

157 calories

4½-in (12-cm) length daikon radish (10 oz/300 g)
½ carrot (1½ oz/50 g)
vegetable oil

1. Wash the daikon and the carrot, and cut into very thin quarter-rounds (see p. 28). Drop them in cold water to crisp. Drain well and sprinkle with a little vegetable oil.

2. Combine all the Dressing ingredients except the *shiso* and blend well. Wash the *shiso*, pat dry, and chop finely. Just before serving, add the *shiso* to the Dressing.

3. Arrange the daikon radish and carrot on a dish and spoon on the Dressing just before serving.

Shiso Dressing

7 Tbsps vegetable oil

2 Tbsps rice vinegar

scant ½ tsp salt

5 *shiso* leaves

Fried Potatoes with Hot Cucumber-Daikon Dressing

Photograph on page 18

Hot Cucumber-Daikon Dressing has a bright, beautiful color and is full of moist, refreshing goodness—just right for the plain and steady potato. Remember that grated dressings tend to deteriorate rapidly, so make this when ready to serve.

1. Wash and peel the potatoes. Cut them in ½-inch (1.5-cm) cubes.

2. To make the Hot Cucumber-Daikon Dressing, peel the daikon radish, punch a hole in its core with a chopstick, and insert ¼ of the red chili pepper (see p. 62). Grate the daikon with the red pepper inserted and squeeze out some of the liquid. Grate the cucumber. Drain. Finely chop the green onion. Chop the remaining ¼ of the red pepper. Combine the daikon radish, cucumber, onion, and red chili pepper in a bowl. Add salt and light soy sauce and mix well.

3. Heat the oil to 320°F (160°C). Dry the cubed potatoes thoroughly with paper towels, and place in the oil. Increase the temperature to 360°F (180°C). Deep-fry the potatoes until they turn a light brown.

4. Add the lemon juice to the Dressing and blend well. Add the fried potatoes, toss, and serve immediately.

Serves 4

85 calories

2 potatoes (10 oz/300 g)

Hot Cucumber-Daikon Dressing

¾-inch (2-cm) length daikon radish (1¾ oz/50 g)

½ red chili pepper

1½ Japanese cucumbers (5 oz/150 g)

1–2 green onions

1 tsp salt

1 tsp light soy sauce

vegetable oil for deep-frying

4–5 tsps lemon juice

Mushroom Salads

Shimeji Mushroom and Spinach Salad

Photograph on page 19

Shimeji mushrooms are simmered briefly to release their flavor while retaining the pleasant texture.

1. Wash the mushrooms, then cut away the ends of the stems. Divide them into small clusters. Combine the Dressing ingredients in a saucepan and place over medium heat. Add the mushrooms and simmer until tender. Remove from heat and let cool to room temperature.

2. Wash the spinach thoroughly. Bring an ample amount of lightly salted water to a boil and blanch the spinach. Immerse in cold water, drain, and gently squeeze out the excess water with your hands or a bamboo rolling mat. Cut the spinach in 1-inch (3-cm) lengths. Sprinkle with light soy sauce and gently squeeze out the excess.

3. Add the spinach to the *shimeji* mushrooms and Dressing. Soak for 5 minutes, drain, and transfer to a serving dish.

Serves 4

48 calories

3½ oz (100 g) fresh *shimeji* mushrooms

Dressing

3 Tbsps *dashi*

1½ Tbsps light soy sauce

1½ Tbsps *mirin*

13 stalks spinach (1 lb/400 g)

pinch salt

1 tsp light soy sauce

Shiitake Mushroom and Daikon Sprout Salad

Photograph on page 19

The fresh, pungent taste of daikon sprouts is ideal with the more complex and rich flavor of sautéed shiitake mushrooms. Add the crunchy texture of potato chips and you have a salad to excite the appetite. The sautéed mushrooms release a stock that combines with the soy sauce for the perfect dressing.

1. Cut the roots from the daikon sprouts. Wash thoroughly, drain, and cut in half. Let stand in a colander to continue draining.
2. Wipe the caps of the mushrooms with a slightly damp paper towel. Cut away the end of the stem. Quarter the mushrooms.
3. Heat the oil in a frying pan and add the mushrooms. Sauté them until tender, remove from heat, and season by sprinkling with the saké and soy sauce.
4. Combine the daikon sprouts and crumbled potato chips in a bowl and toss.
5. Transfer the daikon sprouts and potato chip mixture to a serving dish. Place the mushrooms on top and pour the juice from the mushrooms over the salad. Sprinkle with bonito flakes.

Serves 4
204 calories

1 lb (400 g) daikon sprouts (*kaiware daikon*)
20 fresh shiitake mushrooms (½ lb/200 g)
1 cup coarsely crumbled potato chips
3 Tbsps vegetable oil
2 Tbsps saké
2 Tbsps soy sauce
4 Tbsps bonito flakes

Enoki Mushrooms with Daikon-Cod Roe Dressing

Photograph on page 19

Enoki mushrooms are a no-calorie delicacy. Compared with shiitake or *shimeji* mushrooms, they have a very subtle, light flavor that alone would not stand up to the strong flavor of cod roe. The grated daikon serves as a mediator for this blend of colors, flavors, and textures.

1. Wash the *enoki* mushrooms and cut away the bottom of the stems. Cut them in half and place them in a saucepan. Sprinkle with the saké, place over medium heat, and cook, stirring constantly with chopsticks, until the mushrooms are soft and tender. Remove from heat, drain, and let cool in a colander.
2. Place the green soybeans in their pods in boiling water and cook until tender. Drain. Remove the beans from the pods and carefully remove the thin membrane from each bean.
3. Grate the daikon radish and gently squeeze out some of the water.
4. Make a vertical incision in each sac of the cod roe and use the edge of the knife to gently scrape out the eggs. Transfer them to a bowl, add a dash of saké, and blend well.
5. Add the grated daikon radish to the cod roe and blend thoroughly. Combine the Dressing and the *enoki* mushrooms, transfer to a serving dish, and sprinkle with the green soybeans.

Serves 4
36 calories

10 oz (300 g) *enoki* mushrooms
1 Tbsp saké
8–10 pods green soybeans

Daikon-Cod Roe Dressing
4½-inch (12-cm) length daikon radish (10 oz/300 g)
1 small piece lightly salted cod roe
dash saké

Tofu Salads

Butterhead Lettuce with Miso-Flavored Tofu

Photograph on page 20

Tofu marinated in a miso sauce is paired with fresh greens. A special type of miso know as Kinzanji miso is used in this recipe.

Serves 4
97 calories

You can substitute regular red miso and *mirin* or saké if Kinzanji miso is not available.

1. Wrap the tofu in a non-terry kitchen towel, place it on a cutting board, and weight with 2–3 dinner plates. Set the board at a slight angle and allow the tofu to drain for about 20 minutes.

2. Add the soy sauce to the Kinzanji miso and mix well to form a thin miso paste.

3. Unwrap the tofu and wipe with paper towels. Cut it as you would a loaf in ³⁄₈-inch (1-cm) slices. Spread half of the miso in the bottom of a flat, shallow pan, lay a piece of cheesecloth over the miso, and arrange the tofu in a layer on top of it. Place another piece of cheesecloth over the tofu and spread the remaining miso evenly over the top. Let stand overnight until the surface of the tofu has taken on the color of the miso.

4. Wash the lettuce, drain, and pat dry. Tear it into bite-sized pieces.

5. Remove the tofu from the miso marinade and cut it in ½-inch (1.5-cm) cubes.

6. Combine the tofu, lettuce, and chopped peanuts. Just before serving, pour a little vegetable oil over the salad and toss.

The marinating time for the tofu differs according to room temperature—the warmer, the faster. In warm weather, refrigerate while marinating.

You can flavor the tofu in about 1–2 hours without using cheesecloth. Simply cut it in cubes and mix with the miso. Small amounts of the Kinzanji miso can also be mixed in to flavor the salad.

1 block regular ("cotton") tofu (10 oz/300 g)

²⁄₃ cup Kinzanji miso (½ lb/200 g)

3–5 Tbsps soy sauce

1 butterhead lettuce

3–4 roasted peanuts, coarsely chopped

dash vegetable oil

2 pieces of cheesecloth

Kinzanji Miso: Kinzanji miso (sold as "natto miso chutney") is a traditional Japanese relish that is delectably savory, yet somewhat sweet. This chunky miso is produced by combining soybeans, barley or wheat, vegetables, salt, and other ingredients and fermenting for six months. The Kinzanji miso shown here is made from soybeans, barley miso, *konbu* seaweed, ginger, and barley malt.

Deep-Fried Tofu Salad

Photograph on page 20

Tofu is deep-fried, then topped with salted daikon radish, cucumber, and bonito flakes. This salad takes a little planning to get the tofu to the table hot. Add soy sauce just before eating.

1. Remove some of the water from the tofu by wrapping it in a clean, dry, non-terry kitchen towel, placing it on a cutting board, and setting the board at a slight angle. Weight the tofu with 4–5 plates. Let stand for 2 hours to drain.

2. Cut the daikon radish into very thin quarter-rounds (see p. 28). Add ½ tsp of the salt and rub it into the daikon with your hands. Squeeze gently to remove excess water.

3. Slice the cucumber in very thin rounds. Add the remaining ½ tsp salt, rub it in with your hands, and squeeze out the excess water.

4. Unwrap the drained tofu and cut it in 1–1½-inch (2.5–4-cm) cubes. Heat the oil in a pan until it reaches 360°F (180°C). Wipe the surface of the tofu with a paper towel. Coat all surfaces lightly with flour, tapping off any excess, and immediately immerse in hot oil. The trick here is to work quickly, frying the tofu as soon as possible after dredging. Deep-fry the tofu until it turns a light brown.

5. Wash the *shiso* leaves, pat dry, and spread them on a dish. Arrange the deep-fried tofu on top and on it place first the daikon radish and then the cucumber. Top with bonito flakes.

6. Just before serving, pour a little soy sauce on the salad.

Serves 4

141 calories

2 blocks regular ("cotton") tofu (21 oz/600 g)

4½-in (12-cm) length daikon radish (10 oz/300 g)

1 tsp salt

1 Japanese cucumber (3½ oz/100 g)

flour

vegetable oil for deep-frying

8 *shiso* leaves

2 Tbsps bonito flakes

dash soy sauce

Chilled Tofu

Photograph on page 20

No one denies that tofu is a refreshing, high-protein food, but for those who complain that it is too bland, try adding a little oil or perhaps richly flavorful sesame to the dressing. Likewise, plain white tofu can use a colorful accent. Experiment with simple, bright, vegetable garnishes.

1. Cut each block of tofu in quarters.

2. Wash the squash and slice it in very thin wedges. Then peel each wedge. Cut in 2-inch (5-cm) lengths, and julienne. Bring ample water to boil in a pan, add the squash, and boil it briefly until tender. Drain.

3. Combine all the Dressing ingredients.

4. Parch the sesame seeds and crush by hand (see p. 45) over the Dressing.

5. Wash the lettuce, drain well, and tear each leaf in half lengthwise.

6. Cut the *shiso* leaves in very thin strips.

7. Arrange the lettuce leaves on a dish, then the tofu, and top with the squash. Garnish with *shiso*. Pour on some Dressing before serving.

Tofu is most delicious when eaten the day it is made as it develops a somewhat sour taste after a few days. If the tofu is several days old, boil and chill it before using.

Serves 4
200 calories

2 blocks regular ("cotton") tofu (21 oz/600 g)

½ lb (200 g) squash

Dressing

3 Tbsps rice vinegar

2 Tbsps light soy sauce

1 Tbsp vegetable oil

1 Tbsp white sesame seeds

4 leaves romaine lettuce

4 *shiso* leaves

Soybean Salads

Soybeans and *Hijiki* Seaweed with *Wasabi*-Soy Mayonnaise

Photograph on page 21

From the land come soybeans filled with protein, and from the sea comes *hijiki* seaweed—a veritable treasure trove of nutrients. Together they make a healthy and delicious salad. Since some people object to the distinctive flavor of seaweed, we add a mayonnaise-based dressing seasoned with soy sauce and *wasabi* horseradish to make a winning combination yet more appetizing.

1. Wash the soybeans thoroughly and place them in a large saucepan with about three times their volume of lightly salted water (½ tsp salt to 1⅔ cups/400 ml water). Let stand 8–10 hours.

2. Place the pan with soybeans and soaking water over high heat and bring to a boil. Reduce heat to low and add ⅓ cup cold water. After a moment, again pour in ⅓ cup water, trying not to disturb the beans. Increase heat to medium and boil 1–1½ hours until the beans are tender.

3. Wash the snow peas, remove the stems and strings, and cut them in fine strips. Sprinkle with a little salt and blanch them briefly in boiling water. Drain and fan to cool.

4. Immerse the *hijiki* seaweed in ample boiling water, drain, and sprinkle with vegetable oil.

5. To make the Mayonnaise, place the powdered *wasabi* horseradish in a large bowl, add the soy sauce, and blend. Add the mayonnaise gradually and blend thoroughly.

Serves 4
240 calories

⅓ cup soybeans (1¾ oz/50 g)

salt

3–4 snow peas

5 oz (150 g) restored *hijiki* seaweed (see p. 32)

dash vegetable oil

Wasabi-Soy Mayonnaise

2 tsps powdered *wasabi* horseradish

½ Tbsp light soy sauce

7 Tbsps mayonnaise

6. Transfer the soybeans to the large bowl containing the Dressing, add the *hijiki*, and blend. Arrange the salad in a serving dish and top with snow peas.

Green Soybeans Boiled on the Stalk

Photograph on page 21

Green soybeans are generally sold in the market still on their stalks. They are boiled, stalk and all, and then the soybeans are popped from the pods for a delectable snack. Since they are available fresh only during a brief period in late summer, their flavor has powerful associations with that season for millions of Japanese. Bringing them to the table still on the stalk makes an interesting presentation. All you add is a little salt.

1. Cut off the roots of the soybeans. Wash thoroughly.

2. Cut the stalks as necessary so they will fit in a large saucepan. Rub salt on each pod.

3. Bring ample water to a boil, add the green soybeans and boil for about 10 minutes. (If using frozen green soybeans, add the frozen soybeans to boiling water, and boil for 10 minutes.) Drain. Taste and if necessary, sprinkle on more salt. Fan until cool.

Serves 4
72 calories

2 lbs (900 g) green soybeans on the stalk (or 1 lb/450 g frozen green soybeans)

salt

Noodle and Rice Salads

Japanese-style Spaghetti Salad

Photograph on page 22

Spaghetti is traditionally served with rich, calorie-laden sauces. Here is a lighter, Japanese-style alternative that uses no oil. The flavoring comes from soy sauce; salty, colorful salmon roe; *wasabi* horseradish; and fragrant *nori* seaweed. There are no traditional spaghetti spices, but this is a delicious, satisfying concoction nonetheless.

1. Bring ample water to boil in a large pot, add a pinch of salt, and boil the spaghetti until tender. Drain and sprinkle with a little vegetable oil. Let stand in a colander.

2. Wash the cucumber, cut in 1-inch (3-cm) lengths, and julienne.

3. To lightly toast the *nori* seaweed, pass the dull side over a flame several times. The color will brighten when properly toasted. Cut in very fine shreds. (The easiest way to do this is to first crease the sheet in 1-inch (3-cm) strips and tear it apart, then stack the strips and use scissors to shave slivers from the end of the stack.) If your market carries shredded *nori*, it will save you some work.

4. To make the Dressing, reconstitute the powdered *wasabi* with 2 tsps water (see p. 64). Combine the rice vinegar, salt, and light soy sauce, blend, and add to the *wasabi*. Mix well.

5. Reserve a little of the salmon roe for garnish and blend the rest along with the cucumber into the spaghetti.

6. Transfer the spaghetti to a serving dish, sprinkle some *nori* seaweed and the reserved salmon roe on top. The Dressing is added at the table.

Serves 4
237 calories

½ lb (200 g) spaghetti

pinch salt

dash vegetable oil

1 Japanese cucumber (3½ oz./100 g)

½ sheet *nori* seaweed

Wasabi Dressing

2 tsps powdered *wasabi* horseradish

⅓ cup (70 ml) rice vinegar

¼ tsp salt

1½ Tbsps light soy sauce

4 Tbsps salmon roe

Somen Noodle Salad

Photograph on page 22

Somen are thin Japanese wheat noodles generally eaten chilled as a refreshing summer meal. They are most often served with a simple, soy-based sauce, but here is a variation using oil and rice vinegar.

1. Combine the Vinaigrette ingredients and use a whisk or egg-beater to blend thoroughly.

2. Bring an ample amount of water to a boil in a large saucepan, add the *somen* noodles, fanning them out to separate the strands. Return to a boil and add ¼ cup cold water to the pan. Cook the noodles until tender but still firm (*al dente*). To test, fill a cup with water, remove one noodle from the pot, and drop it in the water briefly. Taste—if the noodles are done, drain and transfer to cold water. Knead the noodles gently to remove the starch, changing the water once or twice. Drain and let stand in a colander. Chop the noodles two or three times with a kitchen knife to reduce them to manageable lengths. Sprinkle with a few drops of the Dressing.

3. Blanch the *wakame* seaweed in boiling water, then immerse briefly in cold water. Drain and wring out any excess water. Cut in 1-inch (3-cm) lengths.

4. Separate the chunks of crabmeat and remove any remaining shell and cartilage. Sprinkle with some Dressing.

5. Fill a large bowl with water and salt it lightly. Place the clams in a colander, set the colander in the bowl, and shake vigorously to wash.

6. Heat the saké in a saucepan over medium heat, add the clam meat, and simmer until cooked through. Be careful not to overcook since they will become tough. Let cool to room temperature.

7. Cut the roots from the daikon sprouts, wash well, and cut into 1-inch (2.5-cm) lengths.

8. When all the ingredients have cooled completely, combine and toss thoroughly. Add the Vinaigrette, blend, and transfer to a serving bowl.

Serves 4
419 calories

Japanese Vinaigrette

⅓ cup (80 ml) vegetable oil

3½ Tbsps rice vinegar

¾ tsp salt

pinch pepper

½ lb (200 g) *somen* noodles

1 oz (30 g) restored *wakame* seaweed (see p. 32)

3 oz (80 g) canned crabmeat

3½ oz (100 g) shucked clams

salt

1 Tbsp saké

100 stalks daikon sprouts (*kaiware daikon*) (⅔ oz/20g)

Somen Noodles: *Somen* noodles are deliciously light, making them especially popular during the hot summer months. Served chilled or as a base for salads, *somen* noodles are refreshing and easy to digest. Good quality *somen* is made by hand, from premium quality wheat flour that has been carefully sifted to ensure a smooth texture.

Kuzu Noodle Salad

Photograph on page 22

Kuzu starch has been used as a health food in China and Japan since ancient times. It is still used today as a thickener in various sauces. Recently *kuzu* starch has become very expensive and has been largely supplanted by *katakuriko* starch, a potato starch. Here *kuzu* has been dried and made into noodles.

1. Use scissors to cut the *kuzu* noodles in 4-inch (10-cm) lengths. Bring 8 cups of water to a boil, add the noodles, and boil 15–20 minutes until tender. Drain and submerge the noodles in cold water to cool. Change the water once or twice.

2. Cut the cucumbers and carrot in 1½-inch (4-cm) lengths and julienne.

Serves 4
159 calories

3 oz (80 g) *kuzu* noodles (*kuzukiri*)

2 Japanese cucumbers (½ lb/200 g)

⅓ small carrot (1 oz/30 g)

Sour Mustard-Sesame Dressing

1 Tbsp ground sesame seeds (see p. 44)

½ tsp reconstituted Japanese mustard (see p. 62)

3. To make the Dressing, combine the sesame seed and mustard in a bowl and blend thoroughly. Add the rice vinegar, salt, brown sugar, and *dashi* and mix well.

4. Drain the noodles.

5. Mix the noodles with the cucumbers and carrot, add the Dressing, and blend. Transfer to a serving dish and sprinkle with slivers of ginger.

3 Tbsps rice vinegar

scant ½ tsp salt

½ tsp brown sugar

3 Tbsps *dashi*

1 Tbsp ginger slivers (⅓ oz/10g)

***Kuzu* Noodles:** *Kuzu* starch is made by pounding and washing the root of a vine to separate the starch from the plant fiber. Then the starch is left in the shade in the winter air to dry. A popular Japanese folk medicine, *kuzu-yu*, is made by mixing *kuzu* starch, hot water, and a little sweetener. *Kuzu-yu* is reputed to be good for colds, headaches, and fever and is also easily digestible. Noodles made with this starch are known as *kuzu-kiri*. They are boiled before eating and are delicious cold. *Kuzu* noodles can be mixed with syrup for a simple dessert or used like saifun noodles.

Rice Salad with Western Vegetables

Photograph on page 23

Like Rice Salad (p. 74), this is a close relative of scattered sushi (*chirashi-zushi*, a colorful mix of ingredients in vinegared rice). The dressing has just a little vegetable oil. It should be used sparingly so the rice is moist but not damp. The trick is to add just the right amount and avoid spoiling the fluffiness of the rice.

1. Wash the rice until the water runs clear. Soak it in 1⅔ cups (400 ml) water for 30 minutes. Combine the Dressing ingredients, add to the rice with the saké, cover, and cook (see pp. 36–37). After the rice finishes cooking, remove from heat and let it stand 10 minutes. Fluff using a rice paddle or wooden spoon in a cutting motion. Transfer to a large wooden bowl or sushi tub and fan to cool.

2. If using fresh corn, steam it until tender and cut it from the cob. For frozen, cook according to package directions and drain well.

3. Remove the stems and seeds from the green peppers, and cut in ⅜-inch (1-cm) squares. Boil these briefly and drain well.

4. Wash the celery, remove the strings, and cut in ⅜-inch (1-cm) cubes.

5. Drain the tuna, break into small pieces, and sprinkle with lemon juice.

6. Wash the lettuce and wrap in a towel. Shake off excess water.

7. Combine the rice with the corn, peppers, celery, and tuna, and blend with a rice paddle. Use a light cutting motion to fluff the rice. Avoid mashing it.

8. Arrange the lettuce leaves in two concentric circles on a large platter and spoon a serving of the salad in the middle of each. In the center of the platter make a pile of cherry tomatoes.

Serves 6

295 calories

2 cups short-grain white rice (11 oz/320 g)

Sushi Salad Dressing

3 Tbsps rice vinegar

1 Tbsp vegetable oil

1 tsp salt

1 Tbsp brown sugar

2 Tbsps saké

⅓ cup fresh or frozen corn kernels (2 oz/60 g)

2 green peppers (½ lb/200 g)

½ stalk celery

4 oz (120 g) canned tuna

dash lemon juice

20 butterhead lettuce leaves

12 cherry tomatoes

Saifun Noodle and Egg Thread Salad

Photograph on page 23

The saifun noodles used here are the Chinese-type made from mung bean starch. They have a lot of body but little in the way of distinctive flavor and thus go well with just about anything. Dress them, sauté them—they are very versatile. There is a Japanese version made from potato starch that must be cooked in a different way. Use either type, just follow the package directions.

1. Wash the cucumbers and slice them in 1-inch (3-cm) lengths. Julienne. Combine all the Dressing ingredients, blend well, and sprinkle a few drops over the cucumbers.

2. Drop the saifun noodles in boiling water briefly. Drain, immerse in cold water, and drain well. Chop with 2–3 strokes of a large knife to cut in easy-to-eat lengths. Place the noodles in a colander and sprinkle with some of the Dressing.

3. Add the salt to the egg and beat lightly. Heat the oil in a small frying pan over medium heat, pour off excess oil, and add the egg. Pour in enough egg to cover the bottom of the pan with a thin layer as if making a crepe. When almost set, turn the omelet and cook the other side briefly. Avoid scorching the surface. Turn out the omelet on a cutting board. Repeat until all the egg is gone. Working with two layers of omelet at a time, roll the omelets up. Press the rolled omelet down slightly with your left hand, and cut off thin threads from the end. Use chopsticks to fluff the egg threads and let air circulate through them.

4. Mix together the cucumbers, saifun noodles, and egg threads. Arrange the mixture on a dish and sprinkle with the remaining Dressing. Crush the sesame seeds in your fingers and scatter them over the noodles (see p. 45). If preferred, the sesame can be lightly chopped.

Serves 4

47 calories

2 Japanese cucumbers (½ lb/200 g)

Dressing

1 Tbsp *dashi*

2 Tbsps rice vinegar

2 tsps brown sugar

½ tsp salt

1 tsp light soy sauce

⅓ oz (10 g) saifun noodles (*harusame*)

1 egg

pinch salt

vegetable oil

½ Tbsp parched white sesame seeds

Seaweed Salads

Three-Color *Tosakanori* Seaweed with Miso-Egg Yolk Dressing

Photograph on page 24

Seaweeds are a rich source of minerals but the majority of them—*konbu*, *hijiki*, and so on—are dark colors that call for dressing up. *Tosakanori*, on the other hand, is not only healthy, but comes in an array of naturally beautiful colors. Combine it with almost any vegetable for a striking salad.

1. Drain the three colors of *tosakanori* seaweed and sprinkle each color with ½ tsp rice vinegar. Let stand 20 minutes. Cut in bite-sized pieces.

2. In a small saucepan, combine the Dressing ingredients and set over low heat. Blend well and heat, being careful not to boil. The mixture should be slightly softer than miso. When heated through, remove and let cool.

3. Wash the celery and carrot. Use a vegetable peeler to shave in very fine pieces. Drop in cold water to curl.

4. Arrange the three colors of *tosakanori* in separate piles on a dish. Decorate with the celery and carrot curls. Serve with the Dressing on the side.

Serves 4

80 calories

10 oz (300 g) fresh *tosakanori* seaweed (3½ oz/100 g each of green, red, and white) (or use dulse)

salt

1½ tsps rice vinegar

Miso-Egg Yolk Dressing

5 Tbsps miso

3 Tbsps rice vinegar

2 Tbsps brown sugar

1 egg yolk

½ stalk celery

⅓ carrot

Hijiki Seaweed with Vinegar-Soy Dressing

Photograph on page 24

Hijiki is noteworthy among the nutritious seaweed family for its high calcium content. Its dark color can be combined with carrots, snow peas, or other bright vegetables for striking salads. This one uses julienned vegetables mimicking the threadlike *hijiki*.

1. Drop the *hijiki* in boiling water briefly, drain, and immerse in cold water. Drain again and let stand in a colander.

2. Beat the egg lightly, add a pinch salt, a pinch brown sugar, and 1 tsp saké, and blend well. Heat the oil in a frying pan and add the egg mixture. Spread it in a thin layer, as if making a crepe, and cook until one side sets, turn, and cook until the omelet is firm but not scorched. Transfer to a cutting board and cut in very narrow strips approximately 2 inches (5 cm) long.

3. Julienne the carrot. Place the carrot in a colander and pour boiling water over it. Drain.

4. Remove the stems and strings from the snow peas. Rub them with a little salt and drop in boiling water. Parboil very briefly. They should still be quite crisp. Drain and cool with a fan. Cut in very narrow strips.

5. Parch the sesame seeds and partially grind them (see p. 44).

6. Combine all the Dressing ingredients and blend thoroughly.

7. In a large bowl, mix together the *hijiki*, egg threads, carrot, and snow peas. Add the Dressing, toss well, and sprinkle with the sesame seeds.

Serves 4

37 calories

5 oz (140 g) restored *hijiki* seaweed (see p. 32)

1 egg

pinch salt

pinch brown sugar

1 Tbsp saké

vegetable oil

1-inch (3-cm) length piece carrot (1 oz/30 g)

1¾ oz (50 g) snow peas

salt

1 Tbsp white sesame seeds

Mild Vinegar-Soy Sauce Dressing

2 Tbsps rice vinegar

2 Tbsps light soy sauce

pinch salt

2 Tbsps *dashi*

Cabbage and *Wakame* Seaweed with Mild Soy Dressing

Photograph on page 24

This salad is based on the contrasting textures of high-fiber cabbage and soft, silky *wakame*. The tiny dried fish (*chirimen jako*) provide a salty accent.

1. Separate the cabbage leaf by leaf. Add a little salt to ample boiling water and then add the cabbage leaves. Boil until tender, drain, and fan to cool. Gently squeeze excess water from the cabbage and cut in ¾ × 1½-inch (2 × 4–cm) pieces.

2. Drop the *wakame* seaweed in boiling water, drain immediately, and immerse in cold water. Drain again and squeeze out excess water. Cut away the tough vein. Cut in pieces that are approximately the same size as the cabbage.

3. Wash the *shiso* leaves, cut them in half lengthwise, and slice crosswise in very thin strips.

4. Place the tiny dried fish in a colander, pour boiling water over them, and let drain.

5. Combine all the Dressing ingredients and blend thoroughly.

6. Mix together the cabbage, *wakame*, and tiny dried fish and arrange on a dish. Pour on the Dressing and scatter the *shiso* on top.

Serves 4

28 calories

10 oz (300 g) cabbage

pinch salt

2½ oz (70 g) restored *wakame* seaweed (see p. 32)

10 *shiso* leaves

2 Tbsps tiny dried fish (*chirimen jako*)

Mild Soy Dressing

5 Tbsps *dashi*

1 Tbsp saké

½ tsp salt

1 Tbsp light soy sauce

SIMPLE SALADS

Avocados	Daikon Radish
Broccoli	Bean Sprouts
Red Radishes	Acorn Squash
Asparagus	Zucchini
Mushrooms	Turnips
Green Onions	Tomatoes
Onions	Potatoes
Celery	Green Peppers
Carrots	Spinach
Corn	Peanuts
Cabbage	Chinese Cabbage
Cauliflower	Okra
Cucumbers	Green Beans
Lettuce	Eggplant

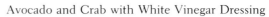

Avocado and Crab with White Vinegar Dressing

Broccoli with Vinegar-Miso Dressing

Avocado and Tuna with *Wasabi* Soy Sauce

90

Radishes with Grated Apple Dressing

Radishes with *Mugi* Miso Dip

Asparagus with Onion Dressing

Asparagus with Vinegared Egg Yolk Dressing

AVOCADOS

Avocados are high in protein and fats. Their rich texture and taste go well with wasabi *horseradish and soy sauce—a kind of avocado "sashimi." The recent popularity of avocado-filled rolled sushi— dubbed "California roll"— is further proof of the appropriateness of this combination. The White Vinegar Dressing used in the first recipe is a delicious tofu and white sesame combination that is also good with the full flavor of avocado. The second recipe pairs avocado "sashimi" with tuna, the most popular kind of sashimi, for one of the richest recipes in this book. The Wasabi-Soy Dressing can of course also be used with avocado alone.*

Avocado and Crab with White Vinegar Dressing

Serves 4
186 calories
2 avocados
dash lemon juice
4 oz (120 g) canned crabmeat

WHITE VINEGAR DRESSING
½ block regular ("cotton") tofu (5 oz/150 g)
1–2 Tbsps lightly parched white sesame seeds
1 tsp rice vinegar
pinch salt
1 tsp light soy sauce
2 tsps brown sugar (or to taste)
½ tsp *mirin*

1. Cut the avocados in half lengthwise, remove the pits and skin. Cut laterally in ½-inch (1.5-cm) slices. Sprinkle with lemon juice to prevent discoloration.

2. Being careful not to break up the crabmeat more than necessary, remove any shell or cartilage.

3. Bring an ample amount of water to a boil in a saucepan. Break the tofu into fairly large chunks and drop it into the boiling water. Continue boiling until the tofu rises to the surface. Drain the tofu into a colander lined with a non-terry kitchen towel and gather the edges of the towel into a bundle. Place the wrapped tofu on a cutting board and weight it with several plates. Let stand about 5 minutes and then gently squeeze out any excess water from the tofu.

4. Place the parched sesame seeds (see p. 44) in a *suribachi* (or mortar) and grind until the seeds begin to release oil. They should form a coarse, sticky paste.

5. Add the tofu to the sesame paste, blend, then continue to grind until well mixed. Add the rice vinegar, salt, light soy sauce, brown sugar, and *mirin*. Mix well.

6. Arrange the avocado slices and crab on a dish and pour on the Dressing.

Avocado and Tuna with *Wasabi* Soy Sauce

Serves 4
224 calories
10 oz (300 g) sashimi-quality tuna
2 avocados
dash lemon juice

WASABI SOY SAUCE
2 tsps reconstituted *wasabi* horseradish (see p. 64)
2 Tbsps soy sauce

shredded *nori* seaweed for garnish (see p. 67)

1. Use a very sharp knife to cut the tuna in ½-inch (1.5 cm) cubes.

2. Slice the avocados in half, remove the pits and skin. Chop them in ⅜-inch (1-cm) cubes and sprinkle with lemon juice to prevent discoloration.

3. To make *Wasabi* Soy Sauce, add the *wasabi* to the soy sauce and mix well.

4. Just before serving, combine the sauce with the tuna and avocado cubes and toss lightly.

5. Mound the salad in individual serving dishes and sprinkle some shredded *nori* on top.

BROCCOLI

Incorporate broccoli into your menus as often as possible as a good source of vitamins A and C. Avoid bunches where the tips have yellowed as this is a sign of age. When boiling, add the tougher stems first—the tender florets need only the briefest cooking.

Broccoli with Vinegar-Miso Dressing

Serves 4
46 calories
½ lb (200 g) broccoli
pinch salt

VINEGAR-MISO DRESSING
2½ Tbsps white miso
1 Tbsp rice vinegar
¼ cup (50 ml) *dashi*

1. Break the broccoli into small florets and wash well. Remove the tough skin from the thicker stalk pieces and cut in ¾-inch (2-cm) lengths.

2. Drop the stalk pieces in ample lightly salted boiling water, cook briefly, and add the florets. When the color brightens, remove from heat and drain.

3. Combine the Dressing ingredients in a saucepan and place over low heat. Stir constantly, being careful not to scorch, until the mixture is smooth and slightly more liquid than miso. Remove from heat and let cool to room temperature.

4. Arrange the broccoli on a serving dish and pour on the Dressing.

RED RADISHES

The bright color and crisp, fresh taste of radishes make them ideal for garnishes or eating raw. But they are also good with Mugi Miso Dip which begins with low-salt miso. Add the slightly sweet taste of mirin and pungent flavor of sesame oil for an ideal dip with any raw vegetable. Try using this dip instead of those with a mayonnaise or sour cream base.

Radishes with Grated Apple Dressing

Serves 4
43 calories
12 red radishes

GRATED APPLE DRESSING
2 apples (10 oz/300 g)
¼ tsp salt

1. Cut the tops from the radishes and wash them thoroughly. Quarter them lengthwise.
2. Peel the apples, grate them finely, and mix in a pinch of salt to prevent discoloration.
3. Combine the radishes and apples and blend. Arrange in a serving dish.

Radishes with *Mugi* Miso Dip

Serves 4
36 calories
12 red radishes

MUGI MISO DIP
2 Tbsps *mugi* miso (see p. 40)
1 tsp *mirin*
1 tsp sesame oil

1. Wash the radishes, tops and all, and pinch off any damaged leaves, saving the best ones to use as decorations.
2. To make the Dip, place the *mugi* miso in a small bowl and gradually add the *mirin* and sesame oil. Mix well.
3. Arrange the radishes in individual serving dishes and serve with the Dip.

ASPARAGUS

Asparagus—or at least the green variety common in Japan and the United States—is high in asparagine, an amino acid said to aid in the prevention of high blood pressure. The lower portions of the stems tend to be tough. Peel them before cooking or reserve them for soup stock. To cook asparagus, bring lightly salted water to a boil and add the asparagus stem first. When tender, drain and fan to cool (see p. 31). The light soy sauce in the Onion Dressing mellows the sharpness of the onion. The color and flavor of Vinegared Egg Yolk Dressing make it a natural for asparagus as well.

Asparagus with Onion Dressing

Serves 4
104 calories
10 spears asparagus (½ lb/200 g)
pinch salt
4 button mushrooms
dash lemon juice
1 tomato

ONION DRESSING
⅛ onion
2 Tbsps rice vinegar
4 Tbsps vegetable oil
1 Tbsp light soy sauce

1. Wash the asparagus and peel the skin from any tough stem ends. Cut it in ¾-inch (2-cm) lengths. Bring ample lightly salted water to a boil, add the asparagus, and boil until tender. Drain and fan to cool.
2. Clean the mushrooms and slice them thinly. Sprinkle with the lemon juice.
3. Chop the tomato in ⅜-inch (1-cm) cubes.
4. Grate the onion and combine with the remaining Dressing ingredients. Blend well.
5. Add the mushrooms and tomato to the bowl with the Dressing and stir gently. Then add the asparagus and toss.

Asparagus with Vinegared Egg Yolk Dressing

Serves 4
62 calories
10 spears asparagus (½ lb/200 g)
pinch salt

VINEGARED EGG YOLK DRESSING
scant ½ tsp *katakuriko* starch (or use arrowroot)
2 tsps–1 Tbsp *dashi* (or water)
2 egg yolks
2 Tbsps rice vinegar
4 tsps *mirin*
¼ tsp salt
scant ½ tsp brown sugar (to taste)

1. Cut the asparagus in half and peel the tough skin from the stem ends. Bring lightly salted water to a boil, add the asparagus, and cook until tender. Drain and fan to cool.
2. Dissolve the *katakuriko* starch in the *dashi*. In a small saucepan, combine the egg yolks, rice vinegar, *mirin*, salt, and brown sugar and the *katakuriko-dashi* mixture. Blend well.
3. Set the pan in a larger saucepan half full of boiling water and stir while heating until the mixture thickens to the consistency of mayonnaise. Be careful not to overheat or boil the Dressing. Remove from heat.
4. Arrange the asparagus on a serving dish and pour on the Dressing.

Button Mushrooms and Green Onions

Green Onion and *Zhacai* Salad

Button Mushroom, Spinach, and Shrimp Salad

Onions with Buttery Mustard-Soy Dressing

Onion and *Wakame* Seaweed Salad

Celery in Soy Sauce

Celery with *Chirimen Jako* Dressing

MUSHROOMS

Mushrooms are nutritious and yet have virtually no calories, making them good diet fare. They are rich in glutamic acid, one of the eight essential amino acids, so use them to bring out the best in salads, sautéed dishes, soups, and so on. In virtually any recipe calling for soy sauce, mushrooms will make a pleasant addition to the flavor combination. Remember that once sliced, mushrooms discolor rapidly, so sprinkle a little lemon juice on them.

Button Mushrooms and Green Onions

Serves 4
43 calories

½ lb (200 g) button mushrooms
dash lemon juice
3 green onions

LEMONY DRESSING
½ Tbsp soy sauce
2 Tbsps vegetable oil
1 Tbsp lemon juice

1. Clean the mushrooms. Use a damp towel to wipe the caps, or wash them if they are particularly dirty. Cut off the ends of the stems and slice very thinly. Sprinkle with lemon juice to prevent discoloration.
2. Cut the roots from the green onions and chop finely.
3. Combine the Dressing ingredients and blend thoroughly with a whisk.
4. When ready to serve, add the mushrooms and green onions to the Dressing and toss well.

Button Mushroom, Spinach, and Shrimp Salad

Serves 4
34 calories

½ lb (200 g) button mushrooms
dash lemon juice
3–5 stalks spinach (3½ oz/100 g)
3½ oz (100 g) shrimp
1 Tbsp saké
dash lemon juice
dash vegetable oil

PINK DRESSING
2 Tbsps rice vinegar
2 Tbsps lemon juice
½ tsp salt
1 Tbsp light soy sauce
1–2 Tbsps ketchup

1. Clean the mushrooms, cut off the ends of the stems, and slice each in quarters. Sprinkle with lemon juice.
2. Wash the spinach well, wrap it in a towel to dry, and cut in 1-inch (3-cm) lengths.

3. Devein the shrimp (see p. 35). Bring ample water to a boil, add the saké, and cook the shrimp. After they turn bright pink, continue cooking for 1 minute at most. Drain and remove the heads and shells (leaving tails intact). Blend the lemon juice and vegetable oil and marinate.
4. Combine the Dressing ingredients and blend well.
5. Pour the Dressing into a serving dish. Combine the mushrooms, spinach, and shrimp, and place on the dish.

GREEN ONIONS

Green onions have a powerful, heady flavor. Combined with dynamic seasonings—particularly typical Chinese ingredients such as zhacai *or sesame—they make interesting and unique salads.*

Zhacai is a Chinese root vegetable generally cured in salt and fiery hot red chili peppers. You may find it preferable to wash and soften the zhacai *to tone it down before using.*

Green Onion and *Zhacai* Salad

Serves 4
24 calories

3 green onions
⅔ oz (20 g) *zhacai*
1 tsp sesame oil
2 tsps parched white sesame seeds

1. Slice the green onions very thinly almost lengthwise, at a slight angle, and drop them in cool water. Drain, wrap them in a towel, and pat dry.
2. Wash the *zhacai* and julienne it in 1-inch (3-cm) lengths.
3. Combine the green onions and *zhacai* and toss well. Just before serving, sprinkle with sesame oil and toss again.
4. Transfer to a serving dish and sprinkle the sesame seeds over the salad as you crush them between your fingers.

Zhacai **(Szechwan preserved vegetable):** This preserved vegetable is a specialty of Szechwan, China. It is made from a type of mustard plant. The root is preserved in salt with chopped hot chili pepper. *Zhacai* comes ready-to-eat in chunks or sliced in plastic bags or cans. If the *zhacai* is too peppery, wash out some of the hot chili flavor before cooking.

ONIONS

It is said that onions help prevent hardening of the arteries and are a tonic for high blood pressure. Meat dishes from various cultures regularly include onion—perhaps not only because they do so much for the flavor of meat, but because of this blood-cleansing property. Other reputed benefits of onions include raising the metabolism and calming the nerves.

Onion and Wakame *Seaweed Salad combines onions with* wakame *seaweed, hard natural cheese, and fragrant* shiso *leaves. The onions help break down the fats and cholesterol in cheese just as they do in meat. The dressing is a fresh lemon and soy mixture.*

Onions with Buttery Mustard-Soy Dressing

Serves 4
67 calories

2 onions (½ lb/200 g)
¼ large purple onion cut crosswise (1¾ oz/50 g)

BUTTERY MUSTARD-SOY DRESSING
2 Tbsps butter (or use margarine)
1 Tbsp soy sauce
½ tsp reconstituted Japanese mustard (see p. 62)

2 tsps chopped green onions

1. Slice the onions and purple onion in thin rounds. Soak in cool water for about 30 minutes. Drain well and arrange on a serving plate.
2. Place the butter in a small saucepan over low heat. When it melts, add the soy sauce and then the mustard and blend until smooth. Remove from heat.
3. While the sauce is still hot, pour it over the onions and garnish with the green onions.

Onion and *Wakame* Seaweed Salad

Serves 4
71 calories

2 onions (½ lb/200 g)
scant ½ tsp salt
1¾ oz (50 g) hard natural cheese
6 *shiso* leaves
1 oz (30 g) restored *wakame* seaweed (see p. 32)

DRESSING
2 Tbsps light soy sauce
1 Tbsp rice vinegar
1 Tbsp lemon juice
1 tsp *mirin*
pinch salt

2 Tbsps bonito flakes

1. Peel the onions and slice in very thin rounds. Sprinkle with salt, and gently rub the salt in the onion. Wrap in a towel and plunge the bundle in cold water to rinse. Transfer to another towel and dry. The onions should still be fairly crisp—dry gently.
2. Cut the cheese in thin 3⅜×1-inch (1×2.5-cm) rectangular pieces.
3. Cut the *shiso* leaves in half lengthwise and then slice in thin strips.
4. Drop the *wakame* seaweed briefly in boiling water, transfer to cold water, drain, and cut in 1-inch (3-cm) lengths.
5. Combine all the Dressing ingredients and blend.
6. Add the onions, cheese, *shiso*, and *wakame* and blend with the Dressing. Transfer to a serving dish and sprinkle with bonito flakes before serving.

CELERY

Ideally, a bunch of celery should be divided for different uses—the larger, tougher outer stalks going to soups or boiled dishes and the tender inner stalks being eaten raw in salads. A particularly appetizing idea for salad is to combine the garden-fresh, delicate taste of raw celery with the tiny dried fish known as chirimen jako *or with bonito flakes. Celery is said to improve circulation and stimulate hormonal secretion.*

Celery in Soy Sauce

Serves 4
22 calories

2 stalks celery
2 Tbsps soy sauce
1 cup bonito flakes

1. String the celery and chop coarsely. Sprinkle with the soy sauce and let stand about 30 minutes.
2. Mix the celery with bonito flakes until the celery is coated and transfer to a serving bowl.

Celery with *Chirimen Jako* Dressing

Serves 4
115 calories

2 stalks celery
3 Tbsps vegetable oil
1½ oz (40 g) tiny dried fish (*chirimen jako*)
2 Tbsps lemon juice

1. Cut the celery in 1-inch (3-cm) lengths and slice very thinly lengthwise. Soak in cool water.
2. Heat the vegetable oil in a frying pan and fry the tiny dried fish until very crisp.
3. Drain the celery, wrap it in a towel, and pat dry. Transfer to a serving dish and pour the tiny dried fish and their frying oil over the celery. Finally, sprinkle with the lemon juice.

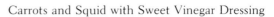
Carrots and Squid with Sweet Vinegar Dressing

Carrots with Sweet Walnut Dressing

Boiled Carrots with Sesame-Mustard Vinaigrette

Corn, Green Soybeans, and Onion with Vinegar-
Soy Sauce Dressing

Cabbage with Mustard-Vinegar Dressing

Cabbage with Simple Pickled Plum Dressing

Furikake Cauliflower Salad

CARROTS

Carrots have abundant vitamin A and enzymes, so raw or cooked they should be a regular part of any healthy diet. They are a good source of energy, especially for anemic people and those who eyes tire easily (although they will not actually improve vision). They are delicious with dressings based on sesame seeds and walnuts. Choose ingredients that bring out the natural sweetness of carrots.

Carrots and Squid with Sweet Vinegar Dressing

Serves 4
136 calories
2 carrots (½ lb/200 g)

SWEET VINEGAR DRESSING
4 Tbsps rice vinegar
4 Tbsps *mirin*
scant ½ tsp salt

2 squid (16 oz/400 g), entrails and tentacles removed
1 Tbsp rice vinegar
¾ tsp finely chopped parsley

1. Wash the carrots and cut them in ¼-inch (5-mm) rounds. Bring ample water to a boil in a saucepan and cook the carrots until tender. Drain and fan to cool.
2. Combine the Dressing ingredients in a saucepan and place over medium heat. Bring to a boil, remove from heat, and let cool.
3. Remove the inner skin of the squid (see p. 34). Cut the squid in ⅓-inch (1-cm) rounds. Bring water to a boil in a saucepan, add the rice vinegar, and drop the squid in briefly. Transfer to cold water. Drain. Be careful not to cook the squid too long since it becomes tough.
4. When the Dressing is cool, add the carrot and squid and mix well. Let stand for 1 hour to allow the flavors to blend.
5. Arrange in serving dishes and sprinkle with the parsley.

Boiled Carrots with Sesame-Mustard Vinaigrette

Serves 4
154 calories
2 carrots (½ lb/200 g)

SESAME-MUSTARD VINAIGRETTE
2 Tbsps rice vinegar
4 Tbsps vegetable oil
½ tsp salt
pinch brown sugar
1 Tbsp partially ground sesame seeds (see p. 44)
¼ tsp reconstituted Japanese mustard (see p. 62)

4 butterhead lettuce leaves

1. Wash the carrots and slice them in ⅛-inch (3-mm) rounds. Bring ample water to a boil, add the carrots, and simmer until tender, but still firm. Drain and fan to cool.
2. To make the Dressing, combine the rice vinegar, oil, salt, and brown sugar and blend thoroughly. Add the sesame seeds and mustard. Stir.
3. Combine the carrots and the Dressing and stir gently to coat thoroughly. Let stand for 30 minutes for the flavors to blend.
4. Line individual dishes with lettuce leaves and add the dressed carrots.

Carrots with Sweet Walnut Dressing

Serves 4
79 calories
2 carrots (½ lb/200 g)
2–3 stalks trefoil (stems only)

SWEET WALNUT DRESSING
1 oz (30 g) toasted walnuts
½ tsp salt
1½ tsps light soy sauce
1 Tbsp *mirin*
½ tsp brown sugar
4 Tbsps *dashi*

1. Wash the carrots and cut them in 1½-inch (4-cm) lengths, then julienne. Bring ample water to boil. Place the julienned carrots in a strainer, lower the strainer into the boiling water, and cook until barely tender. Drain and fan to cool.
2. Drop the trefoil stems in boiling water for a moment, drain, and fan to cool. Cut them in 1-inch (3-cm) lengths.
3. Chop the walnuts finely and place in a *suribachi* (or mortar). Grind well until they form a sticky paste. Use a bamboo skewer to scrape the paste out of the grooves. Combine the remaining Dressing ingredients in a small bowl and blend well. Add this mixture gradually to the walnuts in the *suribachi*, blending to a smooth paste.
4. Add the carrots and trefoil to the *suribachi*, coat well with the Dressing and transfer to a serving dish.

CORN

Though only introduced of late to Japan, corn has an almost uncanny affinity with soy sauce, bonito flakes, and other traditional seasonings. The recipe here is for a salad with Vinegar-Soy Sauce Dressing, but for another simple idea try soy-roasted corn-on-the-cob. Roast the corn until tender, brush on soy sauce, and then return to heat to scorch slightly. The corn retains its wonderful roasted flavor, but the soy sauce brings out even more of the natural sweetness.

Corn, Green Soybeans, and Onion with Vinegar-Soy Sauce Dressing

Serves 4
79 calories

1 cup fresh or frozen corn kernels
1 cup green soybeans in the pod (fresh or frozen)
pinch salt
1 cup coarsely chopped onion

VINEGAR-SOY SAUCE DRESSING
4 tsps light soy sauce
4 tsps rice vinegar

2–3 Tbsps bonito flakes

1. If using fresh corn, steam it until tender and cut from cob. For frozen, cook according to package directions and drain well.
2. Boil the green soybeans in their pods in lightly salted water until tender, drain, and fan to cool. Remove from pods. (If you have extra time and energy, you may want to remove the thin membranes from each bean.)
3. Dip the chopped onion briefly in cool water, drain, and wrap in a towel to dry thoroughly.
4. Blend the Dressing ingredients.
5. Combine the corn, soybeans, onion, and Dressing in a bowl, toss well, and transfer to a serving dish. Top with bonito flakes.

CABBAGE

Cabbage, particularly when eaten raw, is full of fiber and vitamin C—perfect for a healthy salad.

Pickled plums are a good seasoning for cabbage and have the added advantage of aiding the digestion of cabbage. The mild flavor of cabbage also goes well with the flavorful Mustard-Vinegar Dressing.

Cabbage with Mustard-Vinegar Dressing

Serves 4
37 calories

⅙ head cabbage (10 oz/300 g)

MUSTARD-VINEGAR DRESSING
1 tsp reconstituted Japanese mustard (see p. 62)
2 Tbsps light soy sauce
2 Tbsps rice vinegar

1 Tbsp pistachios

1. Wash the cabbage and tear it in 1-inch (3-cm) squares. Soak in cool water.
2. Combine the Dressing ingredients and blend well.
3. Drain the cabbage and wrap it in a towel to dry thoroughly. Add it to the Dressing and toss.
4. Transfer to a serving dish. Chop the pistachios coarsely and sprinkle them over the cabbage before serving.

Cabbage with Simple Pickled Plum Dressing

Serves 4
21 calories

⅙ head cabbage (10 oz/300 g)
2½ Tbsps pickled plum paste (see p. 41)

1. Wash the cabbage and cut it in ½×1-inch (1.5×3-cm) pieces. Place the cabbage in a colander, immerse in boiling water for several seconds, and remove. Drain and fan to cool.
2. Place the pickled plum paste in a bowl. Squeeze the cabbage gently to remove excess water and add it to the bowl. Blend well.

CAULIFLOWER

Raw cauliflower has a moist, crisp freshness that is a pleasure in itself. It is high in vitamin C. Raw in salads or pickled it makes a nutritious and tasty addition to any meal.

Furikake, a mixture of seasonings—often bonito flakes, nori seaweed, sesame seeds, and so on—sold packaged in Japan, is available in some Asian markets outside of Japan. It is generally sprinkled over hot rice, but it can be put to a variety of other uses and adds a salty, soylike flavor to any dish. Depending on the brand, it can include eggs, tiny dried fish, and so on. Try several to see which suits your taste.

Furikake Cauliflower Salad

Serves 4
31 calories

½ head cauliflower (10 oz/300 g)
dash vegetable oil
furikake (as desired)

1. Break the cauliflower into small florets, wash well, and wrap in a towel to dry thoroughly.
2. Use a pastry brush to cover the cauliflower with a thin coat of vegetable oil and sprinkle with *furikake*.

Furikake: Many kinds of *furikake* are sold in Asian markets and natural food stores. One of the most delicious types is the blend shown here (sold as "goma miso furikake") and made of barley miso, green seaweed flakes, and parched sesame seeds.

Korean-style Marinated Cucumbers

Lettuce, *Wakame* Seaweed, and Grapefruit Salad

Cucumber with Red Miso Dressing

Daikon Radish and Carrot Salad

Daikon Radish with *Wakame* Seaweed and Lemon

Daikon Radish and Sprout Salad

CUCUMBERS

Japanese cucumbers are shorter and thinner than the variety commonly sold in the West, and have thinner skin and smaller seeds. They are sweet and mild and go well with virtually any dressing as well as a variety of seaweeds and vegetables.

Cucumbers are said to draw heat from the body and are often used as cold compresses. This means that people subject to chills should avoid eating them in quantity. For the same reason, cucumber salads are best in hot weather—the season in which the vegetable ripens.

Korean-style Marinated Cucumbers

Serves 4
40 calories

4 Japanese cucumbers (1 lb/400 g)
½ tsp salt
2 green onions
1 Tbsp sesame oil

1. Slice the cucumbers as thinly as possible—the rounds should be transparent. Gently rub the salt into the cucumbers. Let stand a few minutes. When the cucumbers are soft and flexible, wrap in a cloth and gently squeeze out excess liquid.
2. Finely chop the green onions.
3. Heat the sesame oil in a frying pan, add the cucumbers, and sauté. Add half the green onions (reserve half for a garnish), stir, and remove from heat. Let cool to room temperature.
4. Transfer to a serving dish and sprinkle with the remaining green onions.

Cucumber with Red Miso Dressing

Serves 4
75 calories

2 Japanese cucumbers (½ lb/200 g)

RED MISO DRESSING
1½ Tbsps red miso
1 Tbsp *mirin*
¼ cup *dashi*
1 Tbsp sesame oil

1 Tbsp toasted pine nuts

1. Slice the cucumbers in ¼-inch (5-mm) rounds.
2. Combine the Dressing ingredients except the sesame oil and blend well.
3. Heat the sesame oil in a frying pan and sauté the cucumbers. When they are somewhat cooked but still crisp, add the Dressing and coat the cucumbers. When the Dressing bubbles, remove from heat and let cool.
4. Transfer to a serving dish. Chop the pine nuts coarsely and sprinkle them over the cucumbers.

LETTUCE

While iceberg lettuce is not as nutritious as some other vegetables, it is high in fiber—the value of which we are just now coming to fully understand. Like cucumbers and other vegetables high in water content, it is particularly appetizing in hot weather. Use it with seaweed or root vegetables for nutritious salads. Here a range of ingredients—wakame seaweed, grapefruit, smoked salmon, egg yolk, and so on—are combined for a substantial, interesting salad-meal. For easy digestion, smoked salmon should always be balanced with raw onion, daikon radish, or the like.

Lettuce, *Wakame* Seaweed, and Grapefruit Salad

Serves 4
180 calories

½ head iceberg lettuce
1 grapefruit
⅔ oz (20 g) restored *wakame* seaweed (see p. 32)
1½ oz (40 g) thinly sliced smoked salmon
½ onion (3½ oz/100 g)
pinch salt

DRESSING
2½ Tbsps saké
7 tsps rice vinegar
4 Tbsps vegetable oil
½ Tbsp light soy sauce
¼ tsp salt

1 hard-boiled egg yolk
2 tsps vegetable oil

1. Wash the lettuce well and tear into bite-sized pieces. Wrap in a cloth to dry thoroughly.
2. Peel the grapefruit and remove the thin membranes from each section. Tear each section in about 3 pieces.
3. Drop the *wakame* seaweed in boiling water, drain, and cut it in 2-inch (5-cm) lengths.
4. Cut the smoked salmon into bite-sized pieces.
5. Slice the onion very thinly lengthwise, spread it out in a colander, and sprinkle with the salt. Let stand 10 minutes, then rinse. Drain, wrap in a towel, and dry completely.
6. Heat the saké in a small saucepan over high heat. Once it boils, remove from heat and let cool. Combine all the rest of the Dressing ingredients, blend well, and add to the cooled saké. Use a whisk to blend well.
7. Force the egg yolk through a fine sieve.
8. Combine the lettuce, grapefruit, *wakame* seaweed, salmon, and onion, toss together, and sprinkle with the vegetable oil. Transfer to a colander to drain well, return to a serving dish, add the Dressing, and blend gently. Top with the egg yolk before serving.

DAIKON RADISH

Daikon radish is full of vitamins (particularly C) and enzymes and makes a healthy addition to any diet. Grated daikon aids digestion, and in Japan it is served almost as a matter of course with fish and shellfish because it has properties which eliminate the harmful bacteria occasionally present in seafood. When using grated daikon for a dressing, squeeze out some of the liquid and reserve it. Daikon juice has medicinal value and can be taken in small doses for stomach disorders, coughs, and sore throats.

Daikon Radish and Carrot Salad

Serves 4
53 calories

6-inch (16-cm) length daikon radish (1 lb/400 g)
2 carrots (½ lb/200 g)

DRESSING
⅔ cup (200 ml) water
1 Tbsp salt
2 tsps whole *sansho* pepper
1 red chili pepper
4 Tbsps rice vinegar
1 Tbsp ginger slivers (⅓ oz/10g)
4 Tbsps *shochu* or saké

1. Wash the daikon and carrots and cut in ⅜ × ⅜ × 1-inch (1 × 1 × 3-cm) pieces. Spread them out on a rack and let stand 3–4 hours to dry. This is best done outdoors (though not in· direct sunlight) or in a place where good air circulation will promote the drying process.
2. To make the Dressing, combine the water, salt, *sansho* pepper, and red chili pepper in a saucepan and place over high heat. Bring to a boil and continue cooking 2 minutes. Remove from heat and let cool. When cool, add the rice vinegar, ginger slivers, and *shochu* or saké and blend.
3. Place the daikon and carrot in a dry container with a lid. Pour the Dressing over the vegetables and cover. Marinate at room temperature 1–2 days.

Daikon Radish and Sprout Salad

Serves 4
95 calories

3-inch (8-cm) length daikon radish (½ lb/200 g)
100 stalks daikon sprouts (*kaiware daikon*)
    (⅔ oz/20 g)

SOY VINAIGRETTE
4 Tbsps vegetable oil
2 Tbsps rice vinegar
2 tsps light soy sauce
pinch salt

1 cup bonito flakes

1. Cut the daikon in 1-inch (3-cm) lengths, julienne, and drop in water to bring out crispness. Drain and spread in a colander.
2. Cut off and discard the roots of the daikon sprouts, wash, and cut in 1-inch (3-cm) lengths.
3. Combine the Dressing ingredients and use a whisk to blend well.
4. Toss together the daikon and sprouts and transfer to a salad bowl. Top with bonito flakes. Just before serving, add the Dressing and toss.

Daikon Radish with *Wakame* Seaweed and Lemon

Serves 4
38 calories

4½ (12-cm) length daikon radish (10 oz/300 g)
pinch salt
1 oz (30 g) restored *wakame* seaweed (see p. 32)
½ lemon

SWEET VINEGAR DRESSING
2 Tbsps rice vinegar
2 Tbsps *mirin*
pinch salt

daikon leaves for garnish

1. Wash the daikon and slice it in very thin quarter-rounds (see p. 28). Sprinkle with salt, let stand 10 minutes, and use your hands to squeeze out excess water.
2. Place the *wakame* in a colander and submerge in boiling water. Transfer immediately to cold water and drain. Cut out and discard any tough veins in the *wakame* and cut it in pieces approximately the same size as the daikon.
3. Slice the half lemon in very thin quarter-rounds (see p. 28).
4. Combine the Dressing ingredients and blend.
5. Prepare daikon pinwheels. Cut several 4-inch (10-cm) lengths from the stems of the leaves. Make a series of diagonal cuts in each piece at ⅛-inch (3-mm) intervals, being careful not to slice all the way through the stem. Next, cut a very thin lengthwise strip from the stem piece and drop it in cold water. The stem will curl naturally into a pinwheel.

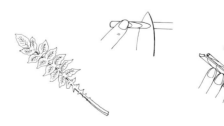

6. Place the daikon, *wakame* seaweed, and lemon in a bowl, toss well, add the Dressing, and toss again. Transfer to a serving dish and garnish with daikon radish stem pinwheels.

Soybean Sprout and Green Pepper Salad

Acorn Squash Salad

Bean Sprouts and Watercress with Pickled Plum
Dressing

Zucchini with Tosa Soy Sauce Dressing

Turnip Chrysanthemums

Turnips and Mangoes with Tofu Mayonnaise

BEAN SPROUTS

The sprouts of beans—mung, soy, and so on—are richer in vitamin C than the beans themselves. They are high in fiber and low in calories, explaining their recent popularity with health-conscious cooks. In China and Japan they have been used since ancient times not only in salads, but in stir-fried dishes and soups. Their roots have a slightly raw flavor and are high in water content. Removing them is time-consuming and tedious, but for special occasions it does make the food less watery and tastier. For everyday use, do not bother.

Be sure to look for very fresh, crisp sprouts. Sprouts, as the name suggests, are the youngest, most precipitously harvested of vegetables. These short-lived nubs of freshness are particularly well balanced by the flavors of soy sauce, miso, or pickled plums whose long curing processes are reflected in rich complex flavors.

Soybean Sprout and Green Pepper Salad

Serves 4
61 calories

10 oz (300 g) soybean sprouts
1 tsp rice vinegar
2 small green peppers

HOT SOY SAUCE DRESSING
1 tsp hot chili pepper oil
2 Tbsps light soy sauce
1 Tbsp rice vinegar
1 Tbsp saké

1. Add the rice vinegar to ample boiling water and blanch the sprouts. Do not overcook them—the texture is one of the virtues of bean sprouts. Drain in a colander, immerse briefly in cool water, and drain well. Chop them in ¾-inch (2-cm) lengths.

2. Remove the stem and seeds from the peppers and cut them lengthwise in thin strips. Drop in boiling water, count to three, and drain. Drop the pepper in cold water and drain thoroughly.

3. Blend all the Dressing ingredients.

4. Combine the sprouts and the pepper, add the Dressing, and toss.

Hot Chili Pepper Oil: This seasoned oil (sold as "hot and spicy sesame oil") is made by frying red chili peppers in sesame oil. The sesame oil turns dark red and takes on the flavor of the red chili peppers. The peppers are removed and the oil is stored in a bottle. Use hot chili pepper oil to give sauces and dressings a spicy touch.

Bean Sprouts and Watercress with Pickled Plum Dressing

Serves 4
37 calories

1 lb (400 g) mung bean sprouts
1 tsp rice vinegar
1 small bunch watercress (3 oz/80 g)

PICKLED PLUM DRESSING
6 pickled plums, with pits (2 oz/60 g) (soaked in water 1–2 hours)
1½ Tbsps *mirin*
1½ tsps soy sauce

1. Wash the sprouts well, and remove the roots if you have the time. Add the rice vinegar to boiling water and blanch the sprouts briefly. Drain, immerse in cold water, and drain again.

2. Wash the watercress and cut off any tough stems. Cut in 1-inch (3-cm) lengths.

3. To make the Dressing, remove the pits from the pickled plums and force the plums through a fine sieve or chop them very finely. Add the *mirin* and soy sauce gradually to thin the pickled plums, and make a smooth thick dressing. If the pickled plums are particularly salty, increase soaking time to 2–3 hours.

4. Combine the sprouts, watercress, and Dressing, and toss.

ACORN SQUASH

Most winter squashes are best stir-fried or sautéed before seasoning. The dressing here uses some salad oil, but it can be deleted. Try substituting other varieties for acorn squash—yellow, butternut, and so on.

Acorn Squash Salad

Serves 4
138 calories

1 lb (400 g) acorn squash

DRESSING
3 Tbsps rice vinegar
4 Tbsps vegetable oil
1 Tbsp light soy sauce

vegetable oil for deep-frying
1 tsp chopped green onions

1. Cut the squash in half and remove the seeds. Slice in very thin wedges.

2. Combine the Dressing ingredients and blend.

3. Heat the oil to 340°F (170°C) and deep-fry the squash until it turns color. (Or sauté until tender—use ample oil.)

4. Drain the squash and add to the Dressing. Toss lightly and arrange in a serving dish. Garnish with green onions.

ZUCCHINI

Zucchini is best when sautéed briefly. The dressing in this recipe is a soy sauce base flavored with bonito flakes. It is usually made separately, but adding the ingredients while sautéing the zucchini brings out and blends the flavors.

Zucchini with Tosa Soy Sauce Dressing

Serves 4
141 calories
2 zucchini (1 lb/400 g)
4 Tbsps vegetable oil

TOSA SOY SAUCE DRESSING
4 tsps soy sauce
⅔ cup bonito flakes

1. Slice the zucchini in ⅛-inch (3-mm) rounds.
2. Heat the oil in a frying pan and sauté the zucchini. When the zucchini is almost tender, sprinkle the soy sauce in the pan and stir to coat well. Then add the bonito flakes, stir through, and remove from heat.
3. Transfer to a serving dish.

TURNIPS

Turnips come in all sizes, from marble to softball and larger; for salads, you want the smallest, freshest ones possible. The large ones have tough fibers and should be reserved for stews and soups.

Turnip Chrysanthemums use a basic Japanese vegetable cutting technique that turns a small white turnip into a chrysanthemum blossom. Adding konbu seaweed to the marinade gives the "chrysanthemums" extra flavor. Turnips and Mangoes with Tofu Mayonnaise is a beautiful white-on-white creation with splashes of orange mango.

Turnips and Mangoes with Tofu Mayonnaise

Serves 4
125 calories
¼ block regular ("cotton") tofu (3 oz/80 g)
2 turnips (½ lb/200 g)
¼ mango (½ lb/200 g)
6–8 pods of green soybeans
3 Tbsps mayonnaise
¼ tsp salt

1. Wrap the tofu in a towel, weight with a plate, and let stand for 30 minutes to drain.
2. Wash and peel the turnips. Cut them in ½-inch (1.5-cm) cubes. Add salt to water (1 Tbsp per cup) and soak the turnips. Place a plate on the turnips and let stand 30 minutes. The turnips will soften and become flexible. Drain, wrap in a towel, and dry thoroughly.

3. Peel the mango and cut it in cubes about the same size as the turnip.
4. Boil the green soybeans until tender, drain, and remove from their pods. If you prefer, carefully remove the thin membrane from each bean.
5. Force the tofu through a fine sieve, then place it in a *suribachi* (or mortar) and grind to a smooth paste. Add the mayonnaise, blend well, and add the turnip and mango. Coat well and taste. Add a little salt if needed.
6. Transfer to a serving dish and sprinkle with the green soybeans.

Turnip Chrysanthemums

Serves 4
9 calories
4 small turnips
⅓ red chili pepper

MARINADE
1 cup water
4 tsps salt

4 chrysanthemum leaves

1. Use a paring knife to cut off the stems and hollow out a small area at the turnip stem ends. Wash well and peel.

2. Place one of the turnips on a cutting board, stem side down. Make vertical cuts at ¼-inch (5-mm) intervals first in one direction and then at a right angle to the first cuts, making a crosshatch pattern. Each cut should stop about ¼ inch (5 mm) from the bottom of the turnip. 2 parallel chopsticks, one on either side of the turnip, can serve as stoppers to avoid slicing all the way through. Repeat with remaining turnips.

3. Remove the seeds from the red chili pepper and chop finely.
4. Combine the Marinade ingredients, blend well, and pour the Marinade in a shallow pan large enough that all four turnips can rest in its bottom. Add the turnips and sprinkle on the red chili pepper.
5. Cover the turnips with a plate and place a heavy weight (4–5 plates will work) on top. Let stand 1–2 hours. When the turnips are soft and flexible, remove them from the Marinade, wash, and thoroughly squeeze out the excess water.
6. Spread the chrysanthemum leaves on a plate, arrange the turnips like flowers on top, and place a small piece of the red chili pepper from the Marinade in the center of each turnip.

Tomatoes and *Wakame* Seaweed with Red Miso
 Vinaigrette

Potato, *Wakame* Seaweed, and Green Pepper Salad

Tomatoes and Tofu with Chinese-style Dressing

Potato and Crab Salad

Green Pepper, Pickling Onion, and Squid with
Mustard-Soy Vinaigrette

Potatoes and Green Beans with Sesame
Mayonnaise

111

TOMATOES

Cool, refreshing tomatoes seem to have been made for hot summer days. They can be paired with virtually any vegetable for a delicious salad. Adding tofu or seaweed makes for balanced nutrition. For adding flavor, the reliable soy sauce or miso work well. Try a Chinese-style dressing with sesame oil in a soy sauce or miso base for a novel touch.

Tomatoes and *Wakame* Seaweed with Red Miso Vinaigrette

Serves 4
141 calories
3 tomatoes (10 oz/300 g)
1¾ oz (50 g) restored *wakame* seaweed (see p. 32)

RED MISO VINAIGRETTE
1 Tbsp red miso
2 Tbsps rice vinegar
4 Tbsps vegetable oil

15–30 stalks daikon sprouts (*kaiware daikon*)

1. Chop the tomatoes coarsely.
2. Drop the *wakame* seaweed in boiling water and then immerse in cold water. Cut away any tough veins and chop the *wakame* in 1-inch (3-cm) lengths.
3. To make the Dressing, place the miso in a small bowl, add the rice vinegar a bit at a time, and blend well. Add the vegetable oil and stir until smooth.
4. Spread the *wakame* in a serving dish. Arrange the tomatoes on top and pour the Dressing over it. Cut the daikon sprouts in ½-inch (1.5-cm) lengths and sprinkle them over the tomatoes.

Tomatoes and Tofu with Chinese-style Dressing

Serves 4
164 calories
2 tomatoes (½ lb/200 g)
1 block regular ("cotton") tofu (10 oz/300 g)
5 *shiso* leaves

CHINESE-STYLE DRESSING
2 Tbsps rice vinegar
4 Tbsps vegetable oil
¼ tsp salt
2 tsps light soy sauce
1 tsp *mirin*
1 scant tsp sesame oil
½ Tbsp parched white sesame seeds

1. Cut the tomatoes in ½-inch (1.5-cm) cubes.
2. Cut the tofu in similar sized cubes. Set them on paper towels to drain. (If the tofu is very fresh, use it raw, but if it is more than a day old, first boil it 2–3 minutes, cool in cold water, and drain.)
3. Coarsely chop the *shiso*.

4. Combine all the Dressing ingredients and whisk them together.
5. Arrange the tomatoes on a dish, arrange the tofu on it, and top with *shiso* leaves. Add the Dressing just before serving.

POTATOES

Potatoes contain a large amount of potassium and when eaten in moderation are said to help prevent high blood pressure. In Japan, a scorched form of potato starch is traditionally believed to be good for intestinal and stomach ulcers.

Potato and Crab Salad uses raw potatoes for extra crispness. Sour Chinese-style Dressing, and Sesame Mayonnaise are all light and soy-flavored. The sprouts and green spots on the skins of potatoes contain a poison called solanine, so avoid these parts.

Potato, *Wakame* Seaweed, and Green Pepper Salad

Serves 4
142 calories
3 potatoes (10 oz/300 g)
2 green peppers (½ lb/200 g)
pinch salt
1½ oz (40 g) restored *wakame* seaweed (see p. 32)

SOUR CHINESE-STYLE DRESSING
4 Tbsps rice vinegar
2 Tbsps light soy sauce
2 Tbsps vegetable oil
½ Tbsp sesame oil
pinch brown sugar
pinch salt

1 tsp parched sesame seeds

1. Peel the potatoes. Cut them in 1-inch (3-cm) lengths and julienne. Place in ample boiling water and boil until somewhat tender but still firm. Drain and let stand in a colander.
2. Wash the peppers and cut in half lengthwise. Remove the stems and seeds and slice in thin strips 1-inch (3-cm) long. Add a little salt to rapidly boiling water and boil the pepper slices very briefly. Drain.
3. Place the *wakame* in a colander and submerge it rapidly in boiling water. Plunge in cold water, drain, and squeeze out excess liquid. Cut it in bite-sized pieces.
4. Combine all the Dressing ingredients and blend using a whisk or egg-beater. Add the potatoes, green peppers, and *wakame* seaweed and toss.
5. Transfer to a serving dish and crush the sesame seeds with your fingers as you sprinkle them over the salad.

Potato and Crab Salad

Serves 4
91 calories

½ lb (200 g) new potatoes
½ tsp salt
2 oz (60 g) canned crabmeat

DRESSING
4 Tbsps *mirin*
4 Tbsps rice vinegar
2 Tbsps *dashi*
½ tsp salt
¼ tsp soy sauce

1. Peel the potatoes and julienne. Sprinkle with the salt and rub it in the potatoes.
2. Break the crabmeat in large pieces and remove any remaining shell and cartilage.
3. Combine the Dressing ingredients in a small saucepan and place over medium heat. The soy sauce is only to add a faint aroma, so use it very sparingly. When the mixture boils, remove from heat and let cool.
4. Wash the potatoes, drop them in fresh, cool water for a moment, and drain. Dry well with a towel and add them to the pan with the Dressing. Add the crab and blend well.

Potatoes and Green Beans with Sesame Mayonnaise

Serves 4
209 calories

3 potatoes (10 oz/300 g)
pinch salt
3½ oz (100 g) green beans

SESAME MAYONNAISE
3 Tbsps ground sesame paste (see p. 44)
1 Tbsp rice vinegar
1 tsp light soy sauce
¼ tsp salt
3 Tbsps mayonnaise

1. Peel the potatoes. Cut them in 1-inch (2.5-cm) long pieces about the same thickness as the green beans. Place in boiling water and cook until tender, drain, and dry with a towel. Sprinkle with a little salt.
2. Remove the strings from the green beans and slice them thinly on the diagonal. Sprinkle with a little salt, let stand 1–2 minutes, and drop in boiling water. When they are tender, drain, and fan to cool.
3. Combine all the Dressing ingredients in a bowl and blend thoroughly.
4. Add the potatoes and green beans to the Dressing and toss.

Green peppers are a good source of vitamins A and C. They have a distinctive and fairly powerful flavor that goes well with Japanese mustard, soy sauce, or miso. But the match goes beyond flavor alone. Peppers are unique in that the "fruit" is a thick skin surrounding a hollow cavity containing only the seeds. The nutritional properties of this unique vegetable are balanced perfectly by those of slowly fermented soy sauce and miso.

Green Pepper, Pickling Onion, and Squid with Mustard-Soy Vinaigrette

Serves 4
218 calories

2 small green peppers (5 oz/150 g)
3–4 pickling onions (3½ oz/100 g)
pinch salt
2 small squid (10 oz/300 g), entrails and tentacles removed
1 Tbsp rice vinegar

MUSTARD SOY VINAIGRETTE
2 Tbsps rice vinegar
4 Tbsps vegetable oil
¼ tsp salt
1 tsp light soy sauce
scant ½ tsp reconstituted Japanese mustard (see p. 62)

2–3 finely chopped *shiso* leaves

1. Wash the peppers and remove the stems and seeds. Slice in very thin rounds. Bring ample water to a boil and drop the peppers in for a few seconds. Drain and fan to cool.
2. Peel the onions and slice them in very thin rounds. Spread them out in a colander and sprinkle with a little salt. Let stand for about 10 minutes; the onions should become somewhat soft and flexible. Rinse them and wrap in a towel to dry.
3. Remove the inner skin from the squid (see p. 34). Cut the squid in ¼-inch (5-mm) rounds. Bring an ample amount of water to boil in a saucepan, add the vinegar and then the squid. Simmer 1–2 minutes—no longer since squid becomes very tough when overcooked. Transfer to cold water to stop the cooking process. Drain and wrap in a towel to dry thoroughly.
4. Combine all the Dressing ingredients in a bowl and blend with a whisk or an egg-beater.
5. Toss together the pepper, onion, and squid and transfer to a serving dish. Pour on the Dressing and top with the chopped *shiso* leaves.

Spinach and Oysters with Mild Ginger-Soy Dressing

Peanuts with Mustard-Soy Dressing

Spinach with Scrambled Eggs

Peanuts with White Miso-Onion Dressing

Chinese Cabbage with Green Miso Dressing

Chinese Cabbage, Apples, and Raisins with Sesame
Seed Vinaigrette

SPINACH

Spinach is rich in vitamin A, iron, iodine, and magnesium, making it a natural blood builder. It also promotes the secretion of gastric and pancreatic juices which make for a good appetite and good digestion. However it is served, it deserves a place as a staple in the health-conscious kitchen. A traditional salad with large quantities of raw spinach is delicious, but raw spinach contains a great deal of oxalic acid, which if consumed in excess can cause kidney stones. As an alternative, try cooked spinach salads such Spinach with Ohitashi *Dressing (p. 43).*

Spinach and Oysters with Mild Ginger-Soy Dressing

Serves 4
103 calories

10 stalks spinach (10 oz/300 g)
½ lb (200 g) raw, shelled oysters
pinch salt

MILD GINGER-SOY DRESSING
2 Tbsps soy sauce
1 Tbsp *dashi*
1 tsp ginger juice (see p. 65)

2 Tbsps vegetable oil

1. Wash the spinach thoroughly. Cut in 1-inch (3-cm) lengths.
2. Wash the oysters in lightly salted water, drain, and rinse (see p. 34). Drain well.
3. Combine all the Dressing ingredients and blend well.
4. Heat 1 Tbsp of the vegetable oil in a frying pan, sauté the spinach briefly until it softens, and sprinkle with a pinch of salt. Transfer to a bowl.
5. Add the remaining tablespoon of vegetable oil to the pan and fry the oysters briefly. If you have any doubt about the freshness of the oysters, cook them thoroughly, but if they are fresh enough to eat raw, avoid overcooking as this makes them tough.
6. While both are still hot, combine the spinach and the oysters. Add the Dressing and transfer to a serving dish.

Spinach with Scrambled Eggs

Serves 4
71 calories

10 stalks spinach (10 oz/300 g)
pinch salt
5 Tbsps *dashi*
2½ Tbsps light soy sauce
2 eggs
2 tsps *mirin*
pinch salt

1. Wash the spinach. Add a little salt to ample boiling water and cook the spinach briefly until tender. Transfer to cold water to stop the cooking process, drain, and use your hands to gently squeeze water from the spinach. Cut it in 1-inch (3-cm) lengths.
2. In a shallow pan, blend together the *dashi* and light soy sauce. Add the spinach and work it a bit with your fingers to absorb the liquid. Let stand 30 minutes. Use a bamboo rolling mat or your hands to squeeze out the excess liquid.
3. Beat the eggs lightly in a saucepan, add the *mirin* and salt, and place over low heat. Cook, stirring constantly with a fork or several chopsticks. When the eggs are set, remove from heat. Do not overcook.
4. Arrange the spinach on a serving dish, and mound the eggs in the center.

PEANUTS

Roasting causes the fats in peanuts to go rancid more quickly, so if using roasted nuts, try to find the freshest ones possible, preferably unsalted. If you have unroasted peanuts in the shell, try boiling them in their red skins and adding them to salads or stir-fried dishes. Both the recipes below make good appetizers or snacks.

Peanuts with Mustard-Soy Dressing

Serves 4
178 calories

1 cup shelled, unroasted peanuts
10 stalks trefoil (1¾ oz/50 g)

MUSTARD-SOY DRESSING
½ tsp reconstituted Japanese mustard (see p. 62)
1 Tbsp soy sauce
½ Tbsp *mirin*

1. Leave the skins on the peanuts. Drop them in ample cool water and set over high heat. When the water comes to a boil, reduce the heat to medium and simmer until the peanuts are tender. Test them after 10 minutes. If done, remove from heat, drain, and let cool.
2. Blanch the trefoil in boiling water for a few seconds. Immerse in cold water, drain, and cut in 1-inch (3-cm) lengths.
3. To make the Dressing, gradually add the soy sauce to the mustard. Add the *mirin* and blend well.
4. Add the peanuts to the Dressing, stir to coat well, add the trefoil, and toss.

Peanuts with White Miso-Onion Dressing

Serves 4
201 calories

1 cup shelled, unroasted peanuts

WHITE MISO-ONION DRESSING

4 Tbsps chopped long onions (white part only)

2 Tbsps white miso

1 Tbsp *mirin*

green seaweed flakes (see p. 72)

1. Put the peanuts in ample cold water and place on high heat. When the water boils, reduce heat to medium and simmer until the peanuts are soft—about ten minutes. Remove from heat, drain, and let cool.

2. To make the Dressing, chop the long onions very finely. In a bowl, thin the miso with the *mirin*, add the chopped onions, and blend well.

3. Add the peanuts and coat well with the Dressing. Transfer to a serving dish and sprinkle with the green seaweed flakes.

CHINESE CABBAGE

The high vitamin C content of Chinese cabbage makes it a good salad ingredient during cold season. Its mild flavor makes it delicious stir-fried, boiled, pickled, or marinated.

When buying a head of Chinese cabbage, pick it up and examine it carefully. A good cabbage is solid and heavy with tightly packed leaves that are gathered together at the ends, not open. The black specks sometimes seen on the white stem portion do not affect the flavor. Unlike many vegetables, large heads with fully developed leaves are tastier than smaller ones.

The tender leaf ends can be used in all sorts of salads. If your first impulse is to pass over the tougher, crunchier, white stem portion, you may be interested in a salad that puts them to delicious use. The Green Miso Dressing begins with a white miso base and adds the deep green of spinach for taste and color that are perfect with pale vegetables. The appealing color of this dressing changes rather quickly when exposed to air, so make it as soon as possible before serving.

Chinese Cabbage, Apples, and Raisins with Sesame Seed Vinaigrette

Serves 4
168 calories

½ lb (200 g) Chinese cabbage (tender leaf part)

1 apple (5 oz/150 g)

pinch salt

3 Tbsps raisins

SESAME SEED VINAIGRETTE

2 Tbsps rice vinegar

4 Tbsps vegetable oil

¼ tsp salt

1 Tbsp partially ground white sesame seeds (see p. 44)

1. Wash the Chinese cabbage and cut it in 1-inch (3-cm) squares.

2. Cut the apple in very thin quarter-rounds and soak in lightly salted water. Drain and wrap in a towel to dry.

3. Wash the raisins, drain, and place them in a small, dry saucepan over high heat. Parch them briefly. The raisins will soon soften. Warming them brings out their sweetness.

4. Combine the Dressing ingredients and blend them well with a whisk or egg-beater.

5. Combine the Chinese cabbage, apple, and raisins and toss well. Transfer to a serving dish and pour on the Dressing.

Chinese Cabbage with Green Miso Dressing

Serves 4
139 calories

1 lb (400 g) Chinese cabbage (white stem part)

1 tsp salt

1 Tbsp rice vinegar

1 Tbsp *mirin*

GREEN MISO DRESSING

5 Tbsps white miso

2 Tbsps saké

1 Tbsp rice vinegar

½ cup (130 ml) *dashi*

3 stalks spinach (3½ oz/100 g)

½ Tbsp reconstituted *wasabi* horseradish (see p. 64)

½ lb (200 g) baby scallops

dash rice vinegar

1. Wash the Chinese cabbage and cut it in ¼ × 2-inch (5-mm × 5-cm) rectangular strips.

2. Sprinkle the Chinese cabbage with salt and pour on enough boiling water to cover. Let stand until the water is cool. Drain well. Combine the rice vinegar and *mirin* and sprinkle over the cabbage.

3. To make the Dressing, place the miso in a small bowl. Add the saké, rice vinegar, and *dashi* and blend until smooth. Place over low heat and stir gently as the mixture warms. When it thickens, remove from heat and let cool.

4. Wash the spinach and blanch it in lightly salted boiling water. Drain and immerse in cold water. Squeeze out the excess water and chop finely.

5. Transfer the spinach to a *suribachi* (mortar) and grind it well. When it becomes a smooth paste, add the miso mixture from step 3 and blend well. Then add the *wasabi* and blend.

6. Place the baby scallops in a strainer, wash with lightly salted water, and drain well. Sprinkle with rice vinegar and drain. Dry with a non-terry kitchen towel if necessary.

7. Squeeze any excess water from the Chinese cabbage and add it to the *suribachi* with the Green Miso Dressing. Add the baby scallops and toss well. Transfer to a serving dish.

Okra with Mustard-Peanut Dressing

Green Beans with Mustard-Soy Dressing

Okra and Radish Salad

Green Beans and Shiitake Mushrooms with Lemon-Soy Dressing

Fried Eggplant with White Miso-Ginger Dressing

Fried Eggplant with Grated Daikon Radish

OKRA

When using okra in a salad, look for small, tender pods, no longer than 2–3 inches. Larger okra have tough skins and should be saved for cooked dishes and soups. Preparation begins by rubbing the surface with salt to remove the fine hairs and soften the skin. Okra can be eaten raw or cooked. Scour with salt and boil briefly, drain and fan to cool.

Okra with Mustard-Peanut Dressing

Serves 4
93 calories

20 small pods okra (½ lb/200 g)
pinch salt
1 Tbsp salted, roasted peanuts

MUSTARD-PEANUT DRESSING
3 Tbsps natural peanut butter or 1¾ oz/50 g peanuts
   (see p. 49)
2–3 Tbsps *dashi*
2 tsps soy sauce
scant ½ tsp reconstituted Japanese mustard (see p. 62)

1. Rub the okra pods with salt and place them in a strainer. Bring ample water to a boil in a pan and lower the strainer into the pan for several seconds. Drain well, fan to cool, and cut the pods in ¾-inch (2-cm) lengths.
2. Chop the peanuts coarsely.
3. Add the *dashi* to the peanut butter a tablespoon at a time to thin it, then add the soy sauce and the mustard and blend well.
4. Add the okra to the Dressing and coat. Transfer to a serving dish and sprinkle with the chopped peanuts.

Okra and Radish Salad

Serves 4
21 calories

20 small pods okra (½ lb/200 g)
pinch salt
5 radishes
2 green onions

VINEGAR-SOY SAUCE DRESSING
2 Tbsps light soy sauce
2 Tbsps rice vinegar

1. Rub the okra pods with salt to remove the fine hairs. Use a strainer to lower the okra into boiling water for several seconds, drain, and fan to cool. Slice the pods in ⅛-inch (3-mm) rounds.
2. Wash the radishes and slice them in very thin rounds.
3. Finely chop the green onions and drop in cold water. Drain and wrap in a towel to dry.
4. Combine the soy sauce and the rice vinegar and stir.

5. Toss together the okra and radishes, transfer to a serving dish and pour on the Dressing. Sprinkle with the green onions before serving.

GREEN BEANS

It is important to pick the most suitable beans for a salad. As with most other vegetables, smaller, younger ones are best. The older ones are tough. Also note that green beans come in stringy and stringless varieties. As pods mature, the beans inside grow and disfigure the pods. Look for slender beans. Mustard-Soy Dressing and Lemon-Soy Dressing are all delicious with green beans.

Green Beans with Mustard-Soy Dressing

Serves 4
18 calories

½ lb (200 g) tender, young green beans
pinch salt
½ tsp soy sauce

MUSTARD-SOY DRESSING
½ tsp reconstituted Japanese mustard (see p. 62)
1 Tbsp soy sauce
½ Tbsp *mirin*

1. Cut the beans in 1-inch (3-cm) lengths. (If they are thick, cut them diagonally in long, narrow pieces.) Rub with salt and let stand 1–2 minutes. Bring ample water to boil and cook the beans until just tender. Drain well and sprinkle with soy sauce. Fan to cool.
2. Combine the Dressing ingredients and blend well. Add the green beans and toss.

Green Beans and Shiitake Mushrooms with Lemon-Soy Dressing

Serves 4
79 calories

½ lb (200 g) tender, young green beans
pinch salt
10 fresh shiitake mushrooms (3½ oz/100 g)

LEMON-SOY DRESSING
2 Tbsps light soy sauce
2 Tbsps vegetable oil
1 Tbsp lemon juice

1 Tbsp vegetable oil
1 Tbsp saké

1. If the green beans have tough strings, remove them. Cut in 1-inch (3-cm) lengths. (If the beans are large ones, cut them diagonally in long, narrow pieces.) Rub with a little salt and let stand 1–2 minutes. Bring ample water to a boil and cook the beans until barely tender. Drain well and fan to cool.

2. Wipe the caps of the shiitake mushrooms with a damp cloth. Cut off the end of the stems and cut in quarters.

3. Combine all the Dressing ingredients and use a whisk or egg-beater to mix well.

4. Heat the oil in a frying pan over high heat. Add the mushrooms, sprinkle with the saké, and sauté until the mushrooms are soft. Add the boiled green beans and stir-fry. Warm through and transfer to a serving dish. While the beans and mushrooms are still hot, pour on the Dressing.

EGGPLANT

Eggplant is another good hot weather vegetable. Even in salads, though, it needs to be thoroughly cooked. First deep-fry or sauté in oil and then season with the fermented flavors of miso or soy sauce. Frying eggplant not only turns it an attractive color, it also removes all traces of the bitterness found in raw eggplant.

The recipes below call for the large Western eggplant, but if the smaller Japanese or Italian eggplants are available you will find them more tender and more delicately flavored. Like cucumbers, eggplants draw heat from the body, so large amounts should not be consumed by those subject to chills.

Fried Eggplant with Grated Daikon Radish

Serves 4
35 calories

2 eggplants
sesame oil for deep-frying
2¼-inch (6-cm) length daikon radish (5 oz/150 g)

DRESSING
½ tsp salt
1 tsp light soy sauce
2 tsps rice vinegar

28 kernels of boiled corn
16 boiled green soybeans

1. Wash the eggplants and cut off the stems. Slice the eggplants in half lengthwise and lay them, skin side up, on a cutting board. Make deep lengthwise incisions at ¼-inch (5-mm) intervals in each half, stopping ⅜ inch (1 cm) from each end of the eggplant. The cuts allow the heat to penetrate and make a pouch for the seasoned grated daikon.

2. Heat the sesame oil to 340°F (170°C) and deep-fry the eggplant. Begin frying skin side down. Turn and fry until done. Drain well.

3. Wash the daikon radish and grate finely. Gently squeeze excess water from the grated radish. Place in a small bowl and add all the Dressing ingredients. Blend well.

4. Arrange an eggplant half on each dish, open the cuts in the center, and place ¼ of the seasoned grated daikon radish in each eggplant. Decorate each with a little corn and a few green soybeans.

Fried Eggplant with White Miso-Ginger Dressing

Serves 4
83 calories

2 eggplants

WHITE MISO-GINGER DRESSING
5½ Tbsps white miso
4 Tbsps *dashi*
1 tsp ginger juice (see p. 65)

sesame oil for deep-frying
1 Tbsp ginger slivers (⅓ oz/10 g)

1. Cut off the eggplant stems and chop them coarsely.

2. Combine the Dressing ingredients in a pan and place over low heat. Warm through, stirring constantly with a wooden spoon, being careful not to scorch the bottom. Remove from heat.

3. Heat the sesame oil in a deep saucepan to 340°F (170°C) and deep-fry the eggplant until cooked through. Drain well.

4. While the eggplant is still warm, add it to the Dressing and coat well. Transfer to a serving dish and garnish with the ginger slivers. This dish is delicious either hot or cold.

INDEX